THE DO-IT-YOURSELF GAME SHOOT

By the same author

Living off the Land
Hides, Calls and Decoys
The Sportsman Head to Toe
Modern Pigeon Shooting
The Shooting Handbook
Stanley Duncan – Founder of The Wildfowlers' Association

THE DO-IT-YOURSELF GAME SHOOT

John Humphreys

David & Charles
Newton Abbot   London   North Pomfret (Vt)

Dedicated to the Game Conservancy, for all they have done for the shooting man

Photographs by Dave Parfitt

British Library Cataloguing in Publication Data

Humphreys, John
   The do-it-yourself game shoot.
   1. Hunting – Great Britain
   I. Title
   799.2′ 13′ 0941   SK185

ISBN 0-7153-8493-7

© Text: John Humphreys 1983
© Photographs: Dave Parfitt 1983

All rights reserved. No part of this publication may be reproduced, stored in a retrieval system, or transmitted, in any form or by any means, electronic, mechanical, photocopying, recording or otherwise, without the prior permission of David & Charles (Publishers) Limited

Photoset by Typesetters (Birmingham) Ltd
and printed in Great Britain
by Redwood Burn Ltd, Trowbridge, Wilts.
for David & Charles (Publishers) Limited
Brunel House   Newton Abbot   Devon

Published in the United States of America
by David & Charles Inc
North Pomfret   Vermont 05053   USA

Contents

1. **Finding your Ground** — 7
   Modern game shooting – a place of your own – arrangements with the landowner

2. **February** — 15
   Potential of the shoot – cover and habitat – head counts – vermin – crops – choosing the guns – finance – part-time keeper

3. **March** — 23
   The guns – feeding sites and feeders – straw – corn – the headquarters – rearing plans

4. **April** — 32
   Vermin control – crows – rooks – moorhens – foxes – stoats – weasels – hedgehogs – rats – cats – mink – the Fenn trap – snares – the trapping line – newsletter

5. **May** — 44
   Vermin – drilling cover crops – spraying – collecting eggs – making release pens

6. **June** — 55
   Traps – weather – pigeons – rabbits – hay-cutting – dogging and flushing bars – rearing with broodies – incubators – teamwork – clay pigeon shooting – dogs

7. **July** — 65
   Siting and setting up release pens – food – wild broods – trespassers – harvest

8. **August** — 74
   Harvest – straw – ex-laying pen birds – tags and rings – releasing poults – feather-pecking – automatic feeders

9. **September** — 83
   Duck – corn – beaters – dog-men – insurance – shooting dates – driving – food and water

10	**October**	**93**
	Working party for pens – the first shoot – partridge driving – flags – portable butts – transport – pegs – lunch – acorns – potato harvest – game diary and vermin book	
11	**November**	**103**
	Feed corn – conservation – the pheasant shoot – the shoot supper – handling game – game card – guests – safety	
12	**December**	**116**
	Stops – cocks only – poachers – alarm guns – straying – gratuities – Boxing Day shoot – wildfowl – various	
13	**January**	**126**
	Feeding – cock shooting – the shoot social – planning next season	

Appendices

1	Gilbertson and Page Limited	**130**
2	The Game Conservancy	**130**
3	Monthly Newsletter	**131**
4	Automatic Feeders	**132**
5	Bags on Duke's Ground Shoot	**137**
6	Balance Sheet	**138**
7	The Shoot Secretary	**138**

Further Reading   **140**

Index   **141**

1
Finding your Ground

Modern game shooting – a place of your own – arrangements with the landowner

Shotgun shooting has rarely been a more popular sport than it is today. There was a time when it was the almost exclusive prerogative of the well-to-do and owners of great estates. The coastal wildfowler was one of the few examples of bird shooting by the working man, but in many cases these gunners were semi-professional, while those amateurs who sought their sport on the saltings were regarded as eccentric.

As time passed and the great estates were broken up, more farmers found themselves with game rights in hand. A boom in agriculture made the small farm a viable unit and the farmer had more time to enjoy his field sports. Another factor in the popularisation of the sport was the ease with which it became possible to rear pheasants. The days of an army of keepers collecting ants' eggs, chopping up thousands of hard-boiled eggs and mincing rabbit meat to feed their chicks were made obsolete by the emergence of high-protein pellets of various sizes and blends which fed the tiniest chicks to laying pen hens with ease and convenience. Anyone could be an amateur keeper and the cloud of mystique which the professional keeper had allowed to conceal his arts was blown away. A few pheasants on the back lawn could be reared to maturity by any shooting man with a smattering of commonsense and the right equipment.

Another myth which was exploded in the post-war years was that country sports were the prerogative of country people. Men and women from the towns, now mobile, better informed and with more leisure time, cast their eyes upon the countryside as their playground. Coarse anglers had already shown the way. Every weekend coaches of them left the industrial towns and fished rivers entirely remote from their daily surroundings. Now the ramblers, hikers, bird watchers, sailors and campers followed suit. In time, the shooting man joined the exodus and discovered that, for a price, he could enjoy top-class game shooting of a type once reserved for the landed gentry. The invasion was not always welcomed by the countryman, who saw his peace disrupted every weekend and his fields and banksides speckled with litter. Wise ones capitalised upon it; others tried to educate the invading army to a different set of rules, but no one could halt its advance.

As far as shooting was concerned, the demand soon began to outstrip the supply. A wealthy and leisured professional and working population cast its eyes further and further afield, looking for anything to shoot. Even pigeon and vermin shooting became pricey and highly sought-after; both were activities which the farmer would once have begged you to perform and would have even paid you in cash or cartridges. Pheasant and grouse shooting rocketed in cost as inflation spiralled upwards. A week's grouse shooting for a team of guns now costs many thousands of pounds; a day's pheasant shooting on a great estate requires the equivalent of what was, in the 1940s, a year's salary. A gun in a moderate driven game shoot in the shires, giving ten days' driven shooting and an average bag of 150 head per day, costs well into four figures. The price increases almost by the year.

The result was, not unnaturally, that once again it was only the very wealthy who could afford the driven game shoot and all the sophisticated machinery which went with it. Rent, a keeper's wages, clothing, telephones, transport, rearing costs, the hire of beaters and the purchase of food and equipment all amounted to a pretty hefty annual wage bill. Even so, there seemed to be no shortage of takers.

The less wealthy were obliged to find their sport away from the covertside. Wildfowling became extremely popular, pigeon shooting became a specialised sport in its own right and barren stretches of prairie farmland were snapped up by eager syndicates in the forlorn hope that there might be a pheasant or two in it somewhere. To find a hundred guns to take part in a February hare shoot was easy – the problem was in keeping the number of guns down. The hare shoot was once regarded as little more than a farming chore and guns needed a fair amount of persuading to turn up.

This book is concerned, however, with another category of shooter, also a product of the post-war years, who did not care to disburse the sort of sums necessary for top-class covert shooting but had a preference for the well-shown driven bird over the pheasant walked-up and shot in the behind as it exploded from a hedge bottom. The small rough shoot or minor day with two guns and a pair of spaniels is a wonderful sport in its own right, but the driven bird and the sense of occasion and camaraderie of the more organised shoot represent the summit of sport with the shotgun in Great Britain.

Shooters who yearned after that sort of sport but who could not afford the price, employ a keeper, pay to rear thousands of birds or rent a suitably wooded stretch of mixed farmland had two choices. Either they could go without, dream of what they were missing and offer their services as beaters on the local covert shoot or else they could put shoulder to the wheel and do something positive to redress the situation.

The answer, as this book will show, is to find a piece of ground, gather around you a team of like-minded guns, share the keepering duties and provide your own driven shoot. The cost should be that of rent and the bare essentials. Judicious selection of the guns ought to ensure a balance of skills and access to sufficient of your material needs to see you through a season at the minimum cost. The result might not be a driven shoot of anything approaching classic proportions, but you will all derive as much pleasure and fulfilment from looking after the place and seeing it improve under your stewardship as you will from tackling your very own driven birds of your first shoot.

There is much to do before this dream can be realised and the first and, for many, the hardest part is finding the ground. You

The sportsman preserves the habitat, and with it many animal and plant species which would not otherwise survive

cannot afford to be choosy and, while somewhere like Sandringham would suit your purpose very nicely, you might have to settle for the corner of an old aerodrome with its grassy runways and jumbled piles of broken concrete. Despite the great demand for all forms of shooting, there are still thousands of acres of land, farmed or not farmed, which might be made available for your purposes. It may be that the farmer is not bothered with shooting, that he believes his farm is too small or inhospitable for game birds or that he likes to keep his few wild birds for walking-up himself or even, in some cases, for shooting from his tractor as he drives up and down the rows. Some see their farms as sanctuaries but do not appreciate that properly shot and keepered ground is a better haven than neglected land. The Forestry Commission, various government departments, universities and many other bodies own land and it will be an unlucky searcher whose determination will not eventually be rewarded.

Those with personal connections will always have a better chance than those without. An ear to the ground is useful and a landowner is more likely to give a fair hearing to a suppliant who is known to him than to a stranger. Friends of friends, remote acquaintances and relatives may be used quite shamelessly by the single-minded who is after a bit of shooting. One way is to make yourself known to the local farmers as a safe and reliable pigeon shooter and vermin killer. It is a long apprenticeship, but once you have proved yourself in that way you will be a strong candidate should anything more promising become available.

You will not be able to be particular about the size of the shoot nor its distance from your home. While the greater the acreage and the nearer the better, we are a mobile nation and do not mind travelling for our sport. I know shooters who think nothing of a round trip of three hundred miles for a day's shooting. As for size, the bigger the shoot the better is generally true, but two famous shoots spring to mind as living proof that a small area, properly managed, can give splendid sport. One is the sixty-eight acre shoot run by Will Garfit on the fringe of a Cambridge suburb. By masterly management and close attention to the needs of game, it can produce a hundred bird days, comprising a wide variety of shootable species on the British list. Most shooting men would instantly dismiss the place as too small, but they would be quite wrong. The other example is a tiny shoot of some eleven acres run by Major Archie Coats, the renowned Hampshire pigeon shooter. The shoot is run on the lines of a traditional game shoot with a series of tiny drives and reverse drives on a piece of ground which one might dismiss as being insufficient for a single drive let alone a whole day by conventional standards.

Not many have the gifts of a Garfit or Coats nor the time for shoot management and so a greater margin for error is necessary. I think a minimum area of a hundred acres is required to run a proper shoot, and on poor land with no cover even that might be too small. There is no upper limit to what you might be prepared to take on, but remember that the greater the area, the less likely you will be to acquire it.

Once you have located some possible sites, make a list of them in order of preference and approach the landowner directly. You may simply offer to rent his sporting rights for an agreed sum per acre, and many shoots are run in this way. This means that you will have a substantial sum to find each year but, divided amongst eight or ten of you, this will be less painful and at least you will have somewhere to call your own. An alternative is to offer to run the shooting, keeper the farm, put down some stock and control the vermin. The farmer, in lieu of rent, would have one or two free guns in the venture, guns which he could use as he wished. This is an ideal method as the farmer has free shooting on a well-run shoot which he might have neither the time nor the know-how to manage himself. In addition, he feels he has a stake in the game and will begin to save some tail corn, keep an eye on some rough corners and put a stop to casual poaching.

If you are really lucky, a farmer continually pestered by would-be rough shooters, but with no interest in the sport himself, might let you take over in return for a peppercorn rent, a brace of birds now and then and peace of mind. Believe it or not, some shoots are still run on that basis, and there are probably still some available.

Another ploy, recently gaining momentum, takes the form of some good, old-fashioned bartering. You offer the farmer your services in any area which might appeal to him. I have heard of mechanics offering the maintenance of all farm vehicles in return for shooting, accountants offer accounting, plumbers plumbing and so on. Those unskilled in these areas might try offering their services as a labourer at harvest or other busy times.

I have probably cited enough examples for you to get the general idea; much will depend on the personalities concerned and the nature of the ground as well as many other imponderables. It is important to bear in mind that, while you might suffer many rebuffs, there is plenty of land which will suit you and it is no good sitting at home bemoaning the fact that you cannot get any shooting. Ask yourself just how hard you have really tried.

This book assumes that you have had the good luck and shown the dogged determination to acquire a little shoot which you plan

An enthusiastic team of beaters at Duke's Ground turning a cock pheasant

to make something better than just a place for a Saturday afternoon poke-about. I have based the advice and suggestions on my own experience which includes the acquiring and running of a number of such shoots during my life. Such a shoot which I have recently taken on and which I shall call Duke's Ground will serve as a basis. It is a typical block of farmland in East Anglia, distinguished by its lack of natural cover, huge fields with a small, neglected stock of hardy, wild pheasants and a few inbred partridges. It is one of a group of farms and is surplus to shooting requirements as the 'guvnors' concentrate on the home farms for their sport. Getting the farm was the hard part, but what followed, the collection of a team of like-minded guns, replenishing stocks of birds, establishing cover and pottering about playing gamekeeper, has all been delightful fun – so much so that the raising of a gun and shooting a pheasant is for me no longer the all-important essence of the sport.

The problems encountered and the slow improvement of the shooting holds many lessons which I happily pass on. Their application is, I think, fitting on almost any low-ground farm in the land, and I can see no reason why they might not be applied by any team of keen amateurs. Abandoned airfields, smallholdings, freshwater marshes, neglected reedy bogs – anywhere where a pheasant can find a footing or a duck a splash – can be used. What follows will identify on a month-by-month basis the important considerations.

2
February

Potential of the shoot – cover and habitat – head counts – vermin – crops – choosing the guns – finance – part-time keeper

February marks the end and beginning of the keeper's year and is the time when you might be likely to be taking on your shoot. The rent will be due then, and it is a good time to set in motion the schemes and plans with which your head will be teeming.

The first thing to do is to assess the potential of your new ground and consider the following questions: what sort of farming takes place there, what habitat is there for game, is there any water and what, if any, is the game population? The three essentials for maintaining pheasants are a suitable habitat, the control of vermin and a supply of food. If these three basics are kept in mind, then success is likely.

Make a map of the shoot, marking in any spinneys, copses or abandoned corners. Each one of these is gold dust to you, as it is a nesting site, winter refuge, potential feeding spot and the nub of a possible drive. The more of these there are, the better, but modern farming, with its need for cost-effectiveness, cannot spare many such areas. With modern machinery and chemical fertilisers even the most barren corner can be improved and made to grow barley.

Any spinneys there are will have become neglected, with plenty of spindly tops but very little at ground level where pheasants can shelter from the cold and from prying eyes. The trees will need to be lopped to let in the light. Elder bushes can be chopped half-through and bent over to lie flat on the ground. The tree will put out new shoots from the bole, while the main trunk which you have bent over will continue to live and will provide shelter at ground level. Weeds and grass will grow up through the twigs, die and remain there as further cover. Bald, open patches may be planted with any quick-growing shrubs and trees that you can manage to obtain. Gardeners are often digging out likely bushes which you can use. On Duke's Ground, members of the shoot produced old currant bushes, their family Christmas trees, garden shrubs and a complete lonicera hedge, dug up by the roots and taken down piecemeal. Each of these offerings was lovingly planted; some died, but some grew, and the result was the creation of a small but effective patch of cover which greatly improved one part of the shoot.

An obliging farmer can be most helpful and will not object to you planting cover in forgotten corners. Throughout your enterprise he can make or break your plans and a co-operative one is the best ally you can have. To him you can point out that weedy patch behind the stackyard, the area next to the farm rubbish pit, that point where four hedges meet and into which the combine harvester cannot quite reach, the boggy patch on the bottom field which is so badly drained that the combine got stuck there in the wet summer. Such places occur on many farms and each one can be used as a positive bonus to the shooter. We will look at the drilling of proper cover crops later in the year, but February is the time for tree and bush planting.

A head count of game is easy in this month when cover is sparse. Game birds will be out feeding in the latter part of the afternoon, and a drive or a walk round the shoot with binoculars will reveal the worst. Two or three such outings on sunny days will give you a fairly accurate idea of the game population. Cock pheasants will show up proudly, while the hens will be less conspicuous at this time. On neglected or rough-shot ground, the hen pheasants are shot more often than the wilier cocks, and an overpopulation of cocks will jeopardise the chances of a good breeding season to follow. You will therefore make a mental note to shoot the cocks hard when the time comes.

Partridges will already be in pairs, running along the track at your approach and taking a short flight over into the field. Some of these will be veteran, barren pairs. No new blood will have been introduced for years and partridges are chancy breeders at best, subject to any number of natural and man-made hazards. These old-stagers will also have to be thinned out early in the season, and a pen of new birds introduced. Generally speaking, partridges are a lot of trouble without a full-time keeper. You will have to be content to offer them what protection you can, but leave them very much to their own devices.

On your early reconnaisance you will also be on the lookout for signs of vermin and enemies of game. These are likely to have flourished on neglected ground and it will soon be necessary to eradicate them. Crows' nests in the trees are obvious enough; you will also find rat runs and holes in the hedge bottoms which stoats and weasels will frequent and, if you do the job properly and walk every hedge and ditch, you will find any fox earths that there may be. It is too early in the year for them to be occupied, but you will make a careful note of the places, mark them on your map and return to them in a month or so.

Also on your map you will mark the crops which are to be grown in the various fields. The farmer will furnish you with the information, and the distribution of grass, roots and cereals will give you an overall picture of the shooting potential. Already in your mind will be half-formulated plans for drives, where the beaters will assemble, where you will place the guns and even where the transport might have to wait. The information will also help you to select the points at which to release your reared birds later in the year; they will be less likely to stray if they have a good cover crop nearby. Find out if the farmer is a stubble-burner, enquire about the shooting on neighbouring farms and meet the proprietors. In short, familiarise yourself with every stick and stone.

Now is the time for that most important job of forming your syndicate. The whole venture can be spoiled by a failure to choose like-minded fellow guns. 'Numbers men', who assess a shooting day purely on the size of the bag, are to be avoided; they can never shoot enough, and will not enjoy the modest days which will occur in the formative years of your shoot. Their discontent will spread to the others and you will lose the happy atmosphere which is vital to any sporting occasion. After all, you are out to enjoy yourselves and this aim ought not to be put at risk by one or two malcontents. Experience need not be a consideration, in fact it might even be a drawback. On Duke's Ground we have a number of guns whose previous experience of driven shooting was limited. To them, a driven day with thirty pheasants in the bag was memorable; every shot was relished, every miss agonised over and the occasion approached with a relish and enthusiasm which would have shamed many a hard-bitten, three-day-a-week covert shooter. The newcomers learned quickly, being willing pupils with plenty of incentive, and they soon became positive assets.

As well as having a complete understanding of what you are trying to do, your guns must all be prepared to make a contribution to shoot expenses. This is essential if the costs are to be kept to a minimum. The rent and other outgoings will all have to be paid and an equal share of your estimated budget, plus 10 per cent for contingencies, will have to be paid by all. You will have to decide how many guns your shoot can support. The smaller the ground, the fewer guns you can have, but if you have too few you will not be able to manage your drives properly. Conversely, if you have too many you will be treading on each other's toes and there will not be enough sport to go round. Even the most unselfish shooter requires a few shots in a day to keep him happy.

The extra contributions that the guns can make ought to be a factor in their selection. Those with rearing or keepering experience, good dog-men, farmers with access to seed and machinery, providers of wood and wire, caterers, natural organisers, do-it-yourself experts – all these have qualities upon which you will be able to capitalise. On our shoot, three of the guns live too far away to be able to put in the number of appearances necessary for the round of the amateur keeper. Rather than travel what would amount to many hundreds of extra miles in a year, they prefer to pay a larger fee than the locals, and this money is put directly into the buying of poults. This two-tier type of membership can be tricky as fair treatment must be seen to operate, but this arrangement seems to be an acceptable one and everyone is happy with it. Even so, local men, or those within easy travelling distance, will be more useful to the practical side of shoot management. You can easily assemble them for a working party and they are available to go down and fill up a few feed hoppers whenever they have an hour to spare. The frequent and unpredictable appearance of your guns on the shoot, carrying out various tasks, is also a good deterrent to poachers, dog-walkers and other opportunists.

Duke's Ground, being slightly over a thousand acres comprising large fen fields, supports ten guns. This is a good number to handle; it allows two walking guns on each shoot, provides plenty of labour, is a large enough number between which to share the costs and yet is manageable to transport and small enough to look a tiny band on our sprawling acres. Three guns, as I explained, pay more in lieu of work and this operates very well. The other seven come from all walks of life and contribute a multitude of skills. Jim, for example, farms nearby and is a keen clay man. He has tractors, trailers, tail corn and an agricultural background which is invaluable. His friend Sam runs a plant-hire company and a small farm. He has access to wooden stakes, planks, wire and such useful hardware which, with the help of another member, he makes into release pens and other necessaries. James runs our portable bar and organises the social activities, a very important job. We are also lucky enough to have a full-time gamekeeper as a member and, as a professional, who could be better at overseeing the vermin control and the rearing of a few pheasants? Another gun is a part-time keeper on a large estate and he has numerous contacts for the acquisition of stock birds and corn; in addition, he is an expert with vermin and all matters pertaining to shooting and game preservation.

Time and raw materials are quite as important factors in running a shoot as hard cash. Were we to pay for the time and the items which our guns contribute, it would cost a small fortune and we might be better off to hire a keeper and have done with it! Not only would this defeat the object of the enterprise,

Starting at the bottom on a pheasant shoot

but raise the cost per gun to a level which would not be attractive – one might just as well buy a gun in an established shoot.

A compromise which many small shoots adopt is to engage a pensioner, a retired keeper or a keen but impoverished shooter to do the routine keepering work. Some of those whom I know offer their services for nothing save the odd brace of birds and a drink at Christmas. They do it simply through a love of the sport, and such men are beyond price. I have not been able to find such a one for our shoot, although all my friends with shoots seem to have one if not two of them. You might consider offering a free gun in return for keepering services and this, I know, happens quite often. Such an arrangement might suit a shoot where the guns had limited time to spare. A minor variation is to adopt an eager schoolboy as would-be gamekeeper; they are easy enough to find as a good many boys of fifteen have a keen interest. Show him the ropes, give him a round of feeders to fill and gradually increase his responsibilities. In return, he could be given unlimited pigeon shooting and rabbiting. I could find ten boys tomorrow who would leap at such an opportunity.

However, while all these ways of obtaining cheap labour might seem appealing, it is more fun to involve everyone in doing it themselves. Those guns who are members of expensive syndicates, who see the shoot only on shooting days, who are driven from peg to peg, who know nothing of the nature of the drives, the names of the beaters or the problems of the rearing season, but who just stand by the woodside waiting for the pheasants to fly over them, are deprived of a great deal of pleasure. How can they feel part of the shoot or be involved in the finer points of its strategy? Paid employees see to all that side of things and they sometimes have more fun than their masters, who may be having an off-day, standing by the covertside in a biting east wind.

If that gun has lugged wet straw bales up to the end of a wood to make a feed stack, if he has groaned and sweated with sacks of corn to the same place, if he has nipped his fingers in a Fenn trap, lain awake at night worrying about his poults as a thunderstorm threatens, replenished water troughs from buckets filled from the ditch or performed any of the other myriad tasks necessary for the production of game, then he truly has his money's worth. That man really has a stake in the shoot, feels its successes and failures keenly, and every bird which is shot is a triumph of far more worth than a fleeting feat of marksmanship.

The end of February of your first year on a new shoot should see you with a team of guns, selected by the precepts I have suggested. Try to collect friends, friends of friends or people who are personally recommended. A classified advertisement is a last resort since it is non-selective and you will not find out whether you are suited or not until it is too late. Remember, you are looking for long-term guns who will see the shoot improve from nothing to a respectable, going concern, and you are not looking for a turnover of members.

You will also know the ground well, have a grasp of the farming policy, a note of the cropping plan, an estimate of the game already on the ground, a clear knowledge of the boundaries and an idea of the disposition of the neighbours. On the practical side, you will have planted a few bushes or cuttings in existing belts or woodland, and will have bent down the elders to thicken the cover at ground level.

In future Februaries you will be keeping the feeding stacks full of corn in order to hold your birds on the ground until nesting season, but in your first months this might be too much to manage with all the other things you will have to do. A good team of guns and a familiarity with the farm will represent a good month's work.

3
March

The guns – feeding sites and feeders – straw – corn – the headquarters – rearing plans

Like February, March is a dead month. There might be some faint stirrings of spring on the milder days, but March can be a long, bleak time with natural food at its scarcest, predators sharp-set to snap up the unwary and your few pheasants easily wooed away from your ground to more comfortable quarters where there may be a full-time keeper and regular, heavy feeding. Your team of fellow guns will have been appointed, and it is a good idea to assemble them as soon as possible for some sort of informal occasion, such as a lunch in your house or at the local pub. This will allow people to become acquainted and, if you have chosen wisely, you will find that defences are quickly lowered and the room will be a roar of conversation. If there are long silences with everyone's eyes on their plates, you have cause to worry. With luck, you will be forming relationships which will last far beyond the shooting season and into the years ahead. Friends are the best company in which to shoot. A well-known sportsman once told me that his favourite sport was in places he liked and with people he liked. It is not a bad motto.

At this first meeting you will, as a matter of high priority, arrange for a shoot walk and the establishment of some feeding places. The siting of these is important but not critical. Hungry birds will find food wherever it is, but you will be wise to attract the pheasants towards the middle of the shoot and not out towards the boundaries. Feeders should usually be situated in a little clearing in some sort of cover so that there is protection

Duke's Ground beaters and guns at lunch

from the wind and from prying eyes. Experience will show you the best feeding places, but at this time in your first year be content just to get some established. It is good for morale to get your team straight down to some jobs and even if you have to change some feeding sites later on this early effort will not be wasted. One final point to remember is that feeding places should be accessible by vehicle, unless you have a Land-Rover or four-wheel drive at your disposal. If you have to carry all your straw, corn and other materials across two fields of heavy plough, you might discourage would-be feeders from doing their share. Within a few yards of a farm track is ideal, while on the verge of a major road is obviously unsuitable.

There are two simple ways of creating feeding places, either of which will serve you well. One is the feed stack which uses rubbishy corn and weed seeds which might not run through the holes in a conventional hopper. To make this you simply place a tidy heap of the food in your chosen spot and thatch it with segments of a straw bale. Cut open a bale and break it into a number of slices about four inches thick. Lay these on and around the food, overlapping and covering all the gaps until all the feed is hidden beneath a structure which resembles a thatched hut. Game birds, like chickens, cannot resist a scratch in straw, especially when they suspect that there might be a stray grain left underneath. Your carefully laid thatch will keep out a surprising amount of rain and the corn will be kept dry. This will keep any number of game birds going for a long time. A variation is to make a sort of miniature bale hide as you might for a midget pigeon shooter and simply pour the food inside. Place a sheet of corrugated iron as a roof, with a few bricks to prevent it blowing away, and leave several pop-holes to give access to the birds. Do not put weed seeds down where they will spread onto agricultural land – it will not make you popular with the farmer.

   The other feeding system suitable for good quality corn is the hopper. The galvanised sort with the open trough at the bottom is good for feeding large amounts of corn, but it also feeds large amounts of sparrows and rats. Every sparrow in the area will gather for the feast and it is surprising how much of your precious corn they will scoff. A 5-gallon drum hung from a branch or nailed to a stake is a good, cheap alternative. The bottom of the drum should be about fourteen inches from the ground so that small birds cannot reach it. Cut small holes in the side and bottom, large enough for grains of corn to be pecked through but not so big that it trickles through of its own accord. Cut out the top and make a wooden lid to fit; this should fit snugly and overlap to keep the rain out and be heavy enough not to blow away.

   Rather than cutting or punching out holes, you can make use of the sparrow guards developed and marketed by the Game Conservancy. To fit each unit, simply cut a rectangular opening in the base of your feeding drum and slip the sparrow guard into position. It has a narrow slit through which the corn may be pecked, a grain at a time, and two angled, metal wings which prevent small birds from hovering underneath and stealing the corn. This means that only game birds can eat your precious supplies. We used these excellent gadgets on Duke's Ground and

A simple feed hopper – better than nothing, but not rat- or sparrow-proof

the amount of corn saved was impressive. The tins with holes always had a great flock of sparrows around them, whereas those with sparrow guards were free.

To do the job really well, and in order to cut down on the number of topping-up visits, you can use a 40-gallon instead of a 5-gallon drum. The best large drums are those with fitted, overlapping lids so that they are entirely waterproof. Cut three openings in the bottom of each drum and fit the sparrow guards. Set the drum on breeze blocks so that it stands solidly and squarely with the base about fourteen inches off the ground, fill it with clean corn – no straws or unthreshed ears to prevent it flowing – and this will last a hundred pheasants for a month or more. You will still have to visit it regularly to see that all is well and give it a kick to make sure there is no blockage, but this will only take a few minutes each week. If you paint your tins with heavy-duty bitumen paint, they will last indefinitely and not rust.

Alternatively, professional feed hoppers may be bought from that famous firm of shoot suppliers, Gilbertson and Page of Hertfordshire. (A list of useful items for the amateur keeper available from Gilbertson and Page is given in Appendix 1.) They make feed hoppers of glass-fibre or galvanised steel so that they do not rust, and they come in a variety of sizes. Perhaps one of your guns will buy you a few as part of his contribution. An interesting alternative is the Parsons automatic feeder, which is an excellent aid for the absentee keeper or for the man with one remote, rarely visited shelter belt or a duck pond to feed. The device consists of a large hopper of glass-fibre or metal which stands on four sturdy legs. A car battery powers an apparatus on the bottom which, at a pre-set time or number of times each day, scatters a measured amount of corn or pellets over an area of many square yards.

Whatever type of feeder you employ, be sure to have a good supply of loose straw below and around each. Pheasants love scratching as much as any barnyard fowl, and grain falling in straw is not so accessible to sparrows. Spend an afternoon distributing a few straw bales at each feeding place; these will last you through the spring. Fresh straw bales can be cut open and scattered when the last lot of straw becomes soggy and rotten.

I suspect that very few farms are without a stack of straw bales somewhere about, and I have yet to come across the farmer who did not give the shooting tenant permission to take all he needed. The same applies to corn and you will only need to buy it as a last resort – it is very expensive stuff. If you and your guns do the rounds of all the farmers known to you, you will assemble enough tail corn, sweepings from the bottoms of silos and barn floors, to last you a long time. You must, however, husband it carefully, and ensure that it is all eaten by your game birds and not wasted on sparrows.

As the corn comes in, perhaps half a sackful at a time, you will need a place in which to keep it. It should be stored in 40-gallon drums with close-fitting lids. If you leave it about in sacks, it will attract large numbers of rats. These are worse than sparrows

A Game Conservancy sparrow guard – 90 per cent effective and the best there is

since what they do not eat, they befoul, and they gnaw holes in the sacks, making them useless. Kept in large drums, corn is perfectly safe from these pests and is always there, fresh and clean, when you want it.

Besides your corn, you will need somewhere to keep your stores and the bits and pieces of shoot furniture which, with luck, your guns will be begging, making and buying in readiness for the rearing season. You will also want a base or headquarters, somewhere to meet on shooting days and a place in the dry where you can have your lunch. Ideally, a building can be found which will serve all these purposes. Most farms have some rarely used building or old cart shed which will accommodate you. A place you can lock is ideal, otherwise your equipment will begin to 'walk'. If the worst comes to the worst, you will have to buy a large, second-hand, prefabricated shed, which you can erect on a piece of waste ground by your meeting place. At Duke's Ground we were lucky to be offered the use of some old, indoor pig sties attached to a dilapidated cottage which, in turn, became a rarely used cart shed.

There is a stout, lockable door, plenty of room for all our things and even electric light. The roof leaks and the threat of demolition hangs over it, but to us it has become home. We managed to find a few collapsible tables and some trestle benches – one member bagged a set of Art Nouveau dining chairs – and all this furniture is carried out and set up on the morning of a shoot day in readiness for lunch time in the cart shed. Such a focal point and gathering place is essential on your shoot, and this is the month in which to arrange it with the farmer.

Now is the time to be specific about the areas of responsibility which you are allocating to your fellow amateur keepers. Most important at this time of year is to arrive at a decision about a rearing policy, how many birds you can afford and what age they will be.

The cheapest system is to rear pheasants from the egg, but this calls for a fair amount of costly equipment and someone who can be on call at all hours to keep an eye on the chicks. Really fortunate is the shoot with someone who has both the time and the equipment to do this. Your birds released to cover will cost a fraction of the price of bought-in poults. While few people will have the equipment to deal with large numbers of birds, it is not too difficult for some of you to rear a score or so on the back lawn. An infra-red lamp, a coop, a run and a supply of food will give most people a chance of bringing to maturity at least 70 per cent of their day-olds. Our shoot has one or two such members who proudly produce a cardboard box of poults in the late summer, and they release them with mixed feelings – glad to be

Cocks on the stubble – spring is the best time to count your stocks

rid of the responsibility but sorry to be parted from what have become members of the family.

We have no one member with the time or hardware for a large rearing programme, so we have little choice but to opt for the more expensive alternative of buying poults at six to eight weeks of age. If you pay full game farm prices you will not be able to afford many for your money. However, if you and your members move in keepering circles, you will be able to buy poults at much more favourable rates. Many full-time keepers using modern, high-production methods can easily and cheaply rear large numbers of pheasants and, in a good year, they will have a surplus number of them. Sometimes a keeper is encouraged to use some private enterprise in this way and make himself a little pin money. One of our members has just such a contact and we can buy all our poults at about half game farm prices or, put another way, we can have twice as many to put down as we might otherwise.

Another good ploy is to buy ex-laying pen hen birds. This tactic has many advantages which I shall say more about in

August. The important point for March is that you must decide how many you can afford and place your orders in the right places. Leave it until the last minute and you will find that no one has any left. Order in March and be sure of them.

Buy as many as you can. It is as easy to release a thousand as it is a hundred in terms of man-hours required for their care. In your first year with a run-down shoot you will be looking for every last one. If you can put down a bird an acre, this is ideal, but the cost might limit you to less than that. A bird to two acres would be acceptable, while, of course, every one is better than nothing. The cash is always the limiting factor; we use the supplements from three non-working guns, a share of the other subscriptions plus any outstanding balance from the sale of game. This is enough to buy about five hundred birds of various stages of growth, shape, colour and size. We never reject any.

4
April

Vermin control – crows – rooks – moorhens – foxes – stoats – weasels – hedgehogs – rats – cats – mink – the Fenn trap – snares – the trapping line – newsletter

You will arrive at the beginning of April with a team of guns each aware of his duties, feeding hoppers and straw in likely places, your new shrubs beginning to bud and a number of pheasants booked for later in the year. The invaluable groundwork of familiarising yourself with the layout of the farm and those parts of it especially favoured by game birds will continue. Your farmer should not be neglected and you must find time to explain to him what you are doing. He may know little about shooting and game preservation, could be interested in finding out more and is a useful ally if he is in sympathy with your objectives.

April is the month to begin a systematic campaign against the vermin. Here again the farmer must be kept aware of what is going on – he will not thank you if his dog is caught in a fox wire or if he puts his toe in a vermin trap! There are various ways of approaching the vermin on the shoot. One is to allocate an area of the shoot to a member or, better still, a pair of members of your team. They can be issued with the necessary equipment and given responsibility for one beat. Ideally, one of each pair should have some experience or you must see to it that detailed and strict instructions are given. Alternatively, two keen and experienced members may take over the vermin control on the whole shoot, but should be able to call on the others for assistance, such as driving for a fox or trap checking, as the need arises. What you do not want is everyone setting traps haphazardly so that no one

The carrion crow is one of the worst egg and chick thieves on the shoot

knows what is going on or where the traps are. This is dangerous, wasteful of time and resources and is likely to lead to trouble.

Since man first set his hand to the plough, the ideal concept of the balance of nature began to diminish. The modern countryside is such that predatory species need to be controlled, otherwise they will proliferate at the expense of their victims. While no one would wish to see the last stoat, fox, crow or rat eliminated, overpopulations of them will seriously erode your stocks of game birds. Bear in mind the vital precept that controlling vermin is one of the three major factors in improving a shoot. This is the time to begin to set about it when cover is at its thinnest, predators are becoming more wakeful and mobile with the lengthening days and the game birds are about to start nesting.

Coots and moorhens will eat any food you leave for ducks; they have to be controlled, but only in their open season

Predators which are enemies of game come in both winged and four-legged form. Bird predators which the keeper needs to keep in hand comprise all members of the Corvid family, especially the carrion crow which is a noted and expert thief of chicks and eggs from game bird nests. Crows are said to mate for life but you need to get the pair if you possibly can. They will come to the call or to decoys, but the shooter must be patient and perfectly concealed. No crow ever puts itself anywhere near shotgun range of a human figure. Do not overdo the calling, keep still and you will have a reasonable chance. An ambush beneath the nesting tree is also a good dodge. Destroy all old nests with solid ball or heavy shot in a 12-bore cartridge, so that you will immediately be able to recognise new or repaired nests.

If you have a rookery, you will never have a glut of partridges. Do not exterminate the rooks, for they do a great deal of good, but thin the squabs in early May and make yourself a rook pie. All Corvids are inquisitive birds, and they may be caught in cage traps or letter-box traps, which are simply large, baited cages which are easy to enter but rather more difficult to leave. These can easily be made from scraps of wood and wire, and designs are given in the Game Conservancy's Booklet 3 *Enemies of Game, Part I, Winged Predators.*

Moorhens will steal eggs and game food and may be easily caught in baited traps or flushed and shot. Remember that they have a close season from 1 February to 31 August.

Hawks and owls are protected by law. There is no doubt that they will take a pheasant or partridge chick from time to time – my advice is to let them! I would rather have an owl than a pheasant in a wood and the small number of losses from 'good' predators are but a small sacrifice to make. Remember that you are after a balanced countryside and not the exclusive game farm so beloved of the Edwardians. Sometimes one rogue tawny owl will take over a roosting wood and kill half a dozen poults every night. This is not his fault but yours for overpopulating a wood with pheasants in the first place. This rogue may well have to be dealt with, but it does not mean that all owls are enemies.

Every crow killed saves game nests

Atrocities which have been committed in the name of game preservation in the past are enough to make the blood boil.

Have no mercy on the crow, however, as a pair of crows on the shoot will decimate your stocks. The use of poison in these hard cases is a tricky problem. While it is certainly a highly effective crow-killer, it is fearfully dangerous stuff to use and in inexpert hands can result in the most calamitous disasters. A dog – your own perhaps – has only to lick your bait and it is dead in a few moments. A crow will pick up and carry a poisoned egg many hundreds of yards into who knows whose back garden. There are cases of poisoned eggs being found by children and taken home in the belief that a stray hen had left it there. A smear of the ghastly stuff on your fingers, transferred later to your lunch-time sandwich, could well be the last thing you ever do. Even experienced keepers can make mistakes, and you are only asking for trouble if, as an absentee, amateur keeper yourself, you begin to scatter it about. It is even worse if more than one of your team is up to the same game. There is no need for me to labour the point. A poisoned egg, glued to a piece of wood to prevent its removal, put down one night and taken up first thing next morning represents the absolute limit of use and even then it can be taken as an admission that conventional methods have failed.

The fox in keepered shooting country does great damage to nesting hens and to chicks and poults later in the summer. A vixen feeding cubs is a mighty killer of pheasants and there can be few professional keepers who have not experienced a fox killing mechanically in large numbers and with apparent aimlessness. It is a disaster when such a slaughter takes place in your release pen where your carefully nurtured stock of poults is in residence. You are not a great estate to which the loss of a hundred poults is but a drop in the ocean – they may represent your entire stock.

This is not to be tolerated, and the local hunt must be given due warning that you are taking preventive measures against fox damage. There are plenty of foxes on the ground – some would say too many – and your little enterprise cannot afford to feed them just to keep the hunt happy. I feel that foxes do little

Fox cubs may be appealing, but they must be controlled

damage to game stocks during the winter months; it is only in spring and summer that they will harm you. If there is a local hunt, then keep the foxes down at the high-risk times and leave them alone in the season. No sportsman would happily damage another man's sport, as fox hunters are quick to remind shooters, but the sword is two-edged and cuts both ways. I admire foxes and fox hunting, and feel that any estate without a fox is a poor sort of place, but the pheasants must be protected in their vulnerable stages.

The other main predators are the stoat and the weasel, both good at keeping down rats and mice, but also sudden death for game, especially nesting and hatching partridges. Hedgehogs (now protected) are fearful nest robbers, rats steal and pollute your feedstuffs and will kill quite large pheasant poults in pens, while the domestic cat left to fend for itself is, perhaps, the worst villain of all. A farm cottage on our shoot was deserted last year, and when the occupants moved they left behind them two cats. Almost overnight, it seemed, the two cats became eight. Patches of pheasant feathers and wing bones began to appear on the heap of straw bales where these poachers were accustomed to catch the

A rare event – a stoat and a rabbit caught in the same trap

morning sun. Two determined guns went down twice and managed to mop up the lot.

We are also afflicted, but to a lesser extent, with feral mink, also the descendants of previous escapees. These little beasts are savage and determined killers, are at home in water, rob duck nests and will take a duckling or a fully grown pheasant roosting in a bush with equal ease. Despite my hatred of poison, we used some Cymag down the holes where none but the hole owners would succumb.

For small mammal predators, the Fenn vermin trap is almost universally used, since the once-popular gin trap was outlawed. This trap is a good killer but also a finger-snapper if used by the inexperienced, so get someone to show you how to set and spring it in safety. This trap should be set in a tunnel, natural or man-made, in a place where stoats and rats have their runs. Junctions of hedges, angles in dry-stone walls, under culverts and alongside

Fenn traps should be set in established vermin tracks

fallen trees are likely places. Careful observation will reveal clearly worn tracks which are habitually used and the spots where tracks meet or diverge – the Spaghetti Junctions of the vermin world – and these will be your key places. In time, you will discover sure-fire places for tunnel traps and these will be good killers year after year.

The trap should be set in a spot where a stoat will be tempted to travel – an open, easy runway. You will have left the human taint as little as possible on the trap and the surrounding vegetation. New traps should be left out in the rain or, better still, buried in the garden for a week or two before use. When setting traps around a release pen, reduce the holes at either end of the tunnel so that pheasants will not blunder in and get caught. Nothing is more annoying than to lose precious poults in this way. We lost a few round our portable release pens through this cause. No matter how many twigs we stuck in the entrances of the tunnels to allow only a rat or stoat to pass, the silly birds would force themselves in with suicidal determination. The answer was, of course, to cut a piece of board to fit the end of the tunnel with a neat hole in it through which only a predator could enter.

Fox runs can be similarly identified and a non-self-locking snare (self-locking snares were made illegal under the Wildlife and Countryside Act in 1982) set in an appropriate place. This must, by law, be checked every twenty-four hours. Place some stout sticks above it so that no deer or dog will blunder into it by mistake, and set it in a place where the fox has to go, such as between two tree trunks, in the gap beneath a large, fallen log or on the narrow track worn by your pheasants outside the release pen. Foxes in earths may be bolted by terriers or dug and shot.

In time, you will become an effective trapper and practice will make perfect. There are, however, some important, general rules which must first be mastered. Run your trapping lines on the boundaries of your shoot so that you are maintaining a vermin-free haven within. Wandering rogues, casting covetous eyes on your carefully preserved acres must run the gauntlet of your traps in order to reach their Promised Land. Also, set your traps in a logical progression from one spot to another so that you can easily check them. Deal thoroughly with one area and then move on to the next. When you have identified those key catching spots to which I have referred, just leave traps there and abandon the haphazard, hopeful ones which never seem to catch anything. In this advanced state, your tunnels, which may have started life as drainage pipes or bricks, become natural features, grass-covered, lichenous and part of the landscape.

Most important of all is to inspect all traps and snares daily – twice if you can, but certainly once. The best-set trap or snare is

The kestrel, strictly protected and, in any case, no enemy of game

not always fatal to its victim and leaving any creature to spend hours of mental and physical anguish is not what any field sport is about. Better far to leave the stoats alone – even the blackest-hearted villain deserves a quick, clean death. If you yourself are unable to go, send someone else and make sure he has clear directions as to the siting of each trap. If you are away from home for a few days, then spring all your traps and re-set them on your return.

The Fenn trap is the keeper's friend. It works for him twenty-four hours a day, even when he is asleep, and every head of vermin it kills means more game, more song-birds, more rabbits and more sport when autumn comes. The shoot which deals with its vermin is the one with the game. These brief notes are not intended to deal exhaustively with the subject of trapping and vermin control, but merely to suggest what the amateur keeper should be busy with in April. The Game Conservancy's booklets are excellent on the subject and for a modest price provide a wealth of information of vital interest to the amateur and

Hen mallard with one duckling – not unusual in cold, early springs. She may nest again

professional gamekeeper. A list of useful Game Conservancy booklets is given in Appendix 2.

Establishing a vermin-trapping system which will serve you all the season is a big enough objective for this month. Making tunnels, buying snares and traps and working hard to reduce predators will take you all your time, if, that is, you have got your priorities right.

Even with this great task in hand, I feel it will be a good thing if, before the year becomes too advanced, you can institute a newsletter for all members. Your object here is to hold their attention and commitment during the close season, and to keep everyone in touch with each other's activities. It is easy for the man making pens in his shed at night or the chap doing the round of his feed hoppers or traps to feel that he is the only one doing any work. You, the organiser, are in touch with everyone, and can act as a clearing-house for all the incoming information. The news that a fox has been bagged, a gift of pheasants received or that tail corn is urgently needed can simply be written down and a copy sent to all members, including the farmer. The more you can involve and interest him, the better. Photocopying facilities are available these days to many people, if only in the local library, and while postage is not cheap, the money spent in doing this little exercise every month will not be wasted. I have given an example of one of our newsletters in Appendix 3 to give you the general idea. They are, I should point out, exercises in communication rather than claims to literary merit.

In the second or third week in April, a new phase of your year will begin, for it is then that you will find your first pheasant nest with an egg in it!

5
May

Vermin – drilling cover crops – spraying – collecting eggs – making release pens

You will arrive at your first May actively engaged in trapping, feeding and preserving the habitat on your shoot. You start as you mean to go on and the sooner your guns and your landlord come to think in these terms, the better.

May is the time when the vermin is especially active. Pheasants and partridges will be busy laying eggs, the latter rather later than the former, and predators will be on the hunt for easy meals, the milder weather allowing them to range far and wide. Vegetation is growing well, but it is still low enough for you to mark the runs and see what is going on. The trapping line, time permitting, will be operating all the year round, but May is usually the bumper month when there are few other chores to attend to.

An important consideration this month is the drilling of supplementary cover crops. An important and delicate meeting with the farmer over a cropping plan of the farm will show some possible spots. As a desperate resolve, you can even hire an acre or two here and there, but this can be very expensive as you will have to pay for the value of the corn or other crop that would have been harvested from that land. Duke's Ground is farmed as efficiently and economically as any land I know, being in the heart of the best farmland in England. However, even this farm has some neglected corners in the angles of river banks, in the lee of straw stacks and in abandoned farm cottage gardens. When added together, they amount to a surprising area of land, not worth reclaiming for agricultural purposes but just right for a

Every rough strip on intensively farmed land is a potential drive

little patch of something to hold and protect the pheasants when the farm crops have been harvested. As long as it will not cost the farm anything or be a breeding ground for weeds and plant diseases which could easily spread onto the fields, most farmers will be prepared to allow you to take them in hand.

If you are as lucky as we are, the farmer will even cultivate these patches for you. At his convenience, if the plough is working nearby at the time, your little patches can be turned over in no more than a few minutes and, later on, rotovated. After such kindness, you will hardly have the cheek to ask him to drill it for you too, although a really saintly man might even offer to do that. If your farmer is a member of your syndicate he will do all these things, but you may, at the other extreme, find yourself doing the lot. If the farmer has the time to do none of this, a private arrangement with his tractor driver might be made with the farmer's permission. An alternative is for the gun in your team who is also a farmer to undertake this work. I told you to choose your guns carefully!

At Duke's Ground we operate a compromise. The farmer rotovates our little parcels of land and we take over the drilling and overseeing of the crops. We have tried maize, mustard and kale with some success. All these seeds are cheap to buy. The kale and mustard can be broadcast by hand after a rain shower and they germinate quickly and grow at a remarkable rate. We had a lot of fun with an ancient potato planter, putting a few grains of maize on each cup as it rotated in front of us. This machine set three rows at a time and, despite a poor germination time, the crop grew well and drew practically every pheasant on the shoot. In the thin patches we scattered some rape seed and this, together with the fathen and other weeds which flourished there, created an acre of perfect game cover.

Another good cover crop, handy for odd, isolated corners, is the Jerusalem artichoke. These are notorious at spreading and are hard to eradicate from land in which they have been planted as every little broken chip of tuber will grow again. This means that they should be set near dykes or ditches and in places which are not likely ever to be required for growing other things. The tubers should be dibbed in by hand or simply dropped into furrows left by the plough. Do not set them too thickly or they will grow into an impenetrable jungle too thick for the birds. Rows should be 3ft apart, so that the tall stems will die, partially collapse in the wind and form a warm and secure cover. Snow will fall upon it and the tunnels underneath will remain warm and dry. The cover is permanent and the tubers reproduce themselves. After three or four years, you will be able to dig with a fork and lift a new lot of tubers for planting elsewhere.

Mustard is a popular pheasant cover, being quick-growing and dense. It is susceptible to the frost and collapses and dies after the first prolonged cold spell of winter; however, the dead stalks provide an element of protection even then. Being such a quick-grower, mustard is useful for drilling directly onto the first stubbles revealed at harvest time. A shower of rain will start it growing and it will have reached a height of 3ft in a few weeks.

Mallard in the dykes; they will thrive if vermin is controlled

Strips of mustard or kale are best set along hedges or belts where they provide a fire break as well as giving cover.

One slight problem is that mustard encourages the dreaded potato eel worm, so that sugar beet and potatoes may not be grown on land occupied the previous year by mustard. This drawback is not a feature of the fodder radish. It also grows well and quickly, can be grazed off by stock, behaves as a perennial if sown late enough in the year and is frost- and disease-resistant.

Kale is a popular cover crop and we use the thousand head variety. We broadcast ours, not only because it is easier but also because the pheasants flush from it more gradually, rather than running to the end of the drilled rows and flushing all in a cloud. Sunflowers were once popular, and they add a touch of colour to the summer landscape, but small birds tend to take the seeds almost as soon as they ripen. Buckwheat, canary grass, lupins or even opium poppies are good cover and do especially well on lighter soils. The Game Conservancy offers good advice on cover crops, and it is simply a question of matching the crop to your requirements and to the sort of soil on your shoot. As in most of your plans, the word of the farmer is law, and you should not sow or plant anything without his approval. May is the month to do the job, apart from the drilling of mustard after the harvest.

The farmer will now be spraying his crops against fungoid and insect pests. The shooter will not approve of spraying in principle, and a farmer who sprays heavily should be carefully advised. In this month, when everything seems to be growing like mad, farmers can have a habit of running amok with the sprayer and spraying any patch of greenery which is not a farm crop. This must be discouraged, as the little rough places, the roadsides, dyke banks and anywhere that cow parsley, giant hogweed and stinging nettles flourish are useful to you. Such places do him no real harm in the profit and loss stakes, but to a tidy farmer they are unsightly. The shooter, however, with his eye to the habitat will defend such corners with jealous devotion. Each one is a potential nesting site, a flushing place, a winter refuge and a spot attractive to game birds. A reasonable farmer can be persuaded to spare these, and you must guard them keenly.

Rough dykes in bald landscapes provide nesting sites

If you are to collect eggs for your own hatching and rearing programme, this is the time to do it. On Duke's Ground, as I have explained, we do not have the time, materials or manpower to hatch our own eggs. However, at hay-cutting or silage-making time, when nests full of eggs are likely to be smashed, it is easy enough to collect them. I was once a member of a shoot which grew and cut a large acreage of silage. All the guns came with their dogs just before cutting time and scoured the fields for nests. Eggs were collected, the hen birds spared and given another chance of producing a brood and the dogs were given some unexpected out-of-season work. The eggs thus saved were given to a keeper who put them in his incubator and charged us a small sum for each bird successfully reared or they were hatched by one member who had his own small electric incubator or else someone managed to get hold of a broody hen to put them under. Birds saved in this way were all counted as bonuses and if we

Every rough corner of nettles is a possible nesting site

saved twenty-five we thought we had done well. The real saving, though, was that of the nesting hen bird. Modern silage grows so lush and the cutter travels so fast that with or without flushing bars, very few incubating, ground-nesting birds are spared.

On Duke's Ground we were never too concerned with our own eggs, preferring to put our money into poults. However, game birds often nest in some stupid places, and eggs retrieved from the roadside or places where their likelihood of hatching is nil ought to be collected and placed elsewhere – even if only in another nest of roughly the same age. They will then, at least, have two chances.

Eggs and nests will remind you that your own rearing and releasing programme is approaching, and this is the time to make preparations. You should make a series of pen sections 5×8ft and wired with 1in mesh hexagonal wire. These are quite easy to produce. On our shoot, one member provided the materials and another the labour. By the end of three years, we had enough sections to make two portable release pens large enough for our needs. We had to buy the final roll of wire ourselves, but even so they were cheap pens. Remember to make one section in each pen with a doorway in it, in order to get in and out to service it. One refinement is to have 2ft of the pen at the bottom filled in with boards. This protects the chicks from draughts and also from the eyes of ground predators. Alternatively, sheets of corrugated iron will do, and these have the advantage of allowing you to turn your sections upside-down in alternate years so that you do not always put the same edge to the ground where it is more likely to rot. Ten sections will make a release pen which is easy to erect in an odd corner and will hold enough birds to give you a good drive later in the year. The general rule is that there should be one yard of circumference fence for every bird in the pen, but you will be dealing with short-stay tenants in successive batches and so you can put them in the pens in rather larger numbers.

Pheasant poults in homemade pens. Economise where you can by recycling discarded timber

We were fortunate at Duke's Ground to have an old, established release pen of posts and chicken wire in our one and only spinney. Geographically, it was not situated in an ideal part of the shoot, being rather too near the boundary for my liking, but it had to be where the only woodland lay. This is a fairly large pen and is a useful device to accommodate any birds which you cannot get into your portable pens.

On the principle that it is unwise to place all your eggs in one basket, you should release your birds in more than one place. Put them all in one spot and a fox or a thief can, in one night, ruin your chances for the year to come. This means that it is vital that your pen sections should be made well in advance and this is the time to get the work done. What would you do if your birds arrived before you had the pens in which to house them? Human nature being frail, it might not be enough for the organiser to delegate pen-making and then forget it. Anything might be going wrong, so a check on progress from time to time will not come amiss.

As well as the pens, there are a number of accessories to be procured and prepared. Birds in the pens will need food and water and these essentials will require containers of some sort. The type of feeder already put out in the cover will be useful and will train the birds from a young age to look for and use the distinctive 5-gallon drums. Do not take those you have already established in the cover, despite the fact that they will not be being used by game. Leave them for later in the year when the birds are hungry. Make new ones for the release pens using 5-gallon plastic spray cans, well washed out and fitted with sparrow guards as described in March. A water supply ought to be handy; although it is possible to carry drums of water, it is not to be recommended. Gilbertson and Page drinkers are excellent and, I suspect, already in almost universal use, but buy the biggest you can. Fifty poults, fed on corn and pellets in high summer, will drink a lot of water and the fewer times you have to fill drinkers the better.

Netting for the roof of the pen is an important item which should be bought now and stored out of reach of mice in your

The most modest home-rearing programme will put a few more birds on the shoot

headquarters. Braided nylon is the best sort as it does not rot and will, with care, last for a number of seasons. You will also need some stout posts as supports for portable pens, a supply of the famous, orange baler twine, a bag of grit, a small stock of medicaments, including treatment for gapes, and a general, water-based worming compound. Arrange for a full set of tools, including spade, sledge-hammer, wire-cutters, knife, hammer, nails and staples, to be ready. Prepare a check list of everything you will need for establishing your release pens and assemble the equipment in your headquarters, item by item, so that in July you will be able to take out the lot in one go and know that you are ready for action. May, while your sections are being made, is by no means too early in the year to be doing this.

Our check list reads as follows:

MAY

10 sections of pen	Feed hopper and sparrow guard
5 × 5ft posts	Drinker
Top netting	Gritting tray
4 straw bales	Gilpa poult pellets
8 sheets of corrugated iron	Grit
Orange baler twine	Water
Tools	Fox snare
Nails and staples	4 Fenn traps
Medicaments	Dustbins to store food

If you are employing more than one pen, make the sections up into sets and colour-code each with a dash of paint. This will be a great help when you are sorting out your equipment for the following season. Unless it is obvious, you may delay choosing the actual sites for the release pens until later in the summer.

6
June

Traps – weather – pigeons – rabbits – hay-cutting – dogging and flushing bars – rearing with broodies – incubators – teamwork – clay pigeon shooting – dogs

By now the vegetation will be too thick for you to be able to continue your war on the vermin, but with a bit of luck and the facility to learn quickly, you will have dealt with a number of predators during the earlier months. You will not have been so misguided or vainglorious as to have exhibited a grisly row of your victims on a so-called keeper's gibbet. This was popular years ago when a keeper felt he had to produce visible proof of his efficiency as a vermin killer. Today, passers-by are horrified by such exhibitions and rightly so. Vermin-killing presents one of the less-acceptable faces of shoot management. Vermin should be disposed of quietly and unobtrusively – preferably buried. You will not expect to catch much in June, but keep a trap set in the key spots which you will have discovered. Remember that the rule to check each trap every day should still be strictly applied.

With luck, this month will open with your pens well on the way to completion, birds ordered and strips or patches of your cover crops beginning to show up proudly. June marks that highlight of the social calendar, Royal Ascot, but for the partridge keeper that heady week will hold an even greater significance. It is the time when the bulk of his partridges will hatch and when the fearful thunderstorms which so often mark this time of year will decimate his stocks. The weather is something about which the keenest amateur keeper can do nothing, and he can only watch the skies anxiously and pray. Given a fine week all will go well, and every day thereafter will see the tiny chicks grow in size and strength and thus more rain resistant. You will

Ferreting is an efficient method of controlling rabbits, and adds another dimension to your sporting year

see broods on the farm roads, especially in the evenings and after a shower of rain when the parent birds will bring them out to dry off in the evening sun. Then is the time to drive round quietly in your car and count your chickens – or partridges – after they have hatched.

The corn will be in full ear and the pigeons will have discovered any patches that have been laid by the wind. The birds love the grains when they are in that soft, milky state and will soon establish a beach-head and cause considerable damage to the crop. This is when you can help the farmer and have some sport. If peas, rape or brassicas are grown, pigeons may well have made their presence felt earlier in the year and will be causing your farmer considerable anxiety. Arrange for some of your guns who are versed in the gentle arts of the decoyer to have a few days at the trouble spot. They may kill a lot of pigeons, but even

JUNE

if they do not, it will all be good public relations work and they may even, the modern pigeon being a fickle and flighty creature, drive them away to seek pastures new.

The same applies to rabbits in the early part of the year, and the shooting tenant who helps in this way is not only enjoying good sport, but is also helping the farmer upon whom he depends so much. When pigeon shooting in the summer, remember your game chicks and do not go trampling about in the cover after lost pigeons or, worse still, allow your dog to rampage around on similar missions. Keep to a fixed point, allow the birds to come well in and pick them as they fall. The shooting itself will not create much disturbance and hen birds with chicks will move them quietly away, while pheasants on eggs will sit tight within yards of you. It is all really a matter of common sense.

The first three weeks of June are the most critical time of the year for chick loss. We saw in May how important it was to save nesting hens from the hay and silage cutters. Each hen rescued had the chance of a second brood. Now the second silage and hay cuts are being made, with the tractor and cutter roaring along faster than you can walk. The driver of today is cut off from the world in his sound-proof cab, while his earphones ensure his peace of mind with hour upon hour of pop music. How different

The rabbit is the shooter's friend, but the farmer's enemy

Early rabbiting helps shoot revenue, as well as providing sport

is this from the days when an open Ferguson or Fordson tractor went clanking along, while a straw-hatted man sat on the mower, keeping all his wits about him. Then there was time to stop for a hen and chicks disturbed in the tangle, but modern high-speed and efficient methods have ruled out such considerations. Time is money and game birds have to take their chance.

There are two things the shooter can do at this fraught time which will save some, but not all, of his birds. Most effective is to find out when the field is due to be cut, turn up with all your dog-men and let the dogs loose in the grass. This will drive game birds with chicks out to safer places and will put off the nest the late nesters to spare them a certain death. Keep at it even when the machine is in the field, but see that your dogs are kept away from the cutter otherwise it might be more than a partridge which comes to a sticky end. This is the only practical thing to do in the dense, tall crops which grow on rich land, such as in the Fens. In thinner, shorter grass a flushing bar may be fitted to the front of the tractor. To fit one any further back does not give enough warning, given the high speeds of modern farm machinery. A flushing bar is a piece of stout metal jutting out in front of the mower or silager. Suspended from this at intervals of about fourteen inches is a series of heavy chains which hang down to within a few inches of the ground. The idea is that they will trail along, agitating the grass and disturbing any nesting birds. Both these methods are less than perfect, but at least you feel you are doing something positive to help and not standing idly and impotently by. The flushing bar can be simply made at home or in the farm workshop from a length of angle iron and just bolted on to the tractor.

In May we collected a few eggs from threatened nests and either traded them for poults to be delivered later or passed them to a gun who wished to try his hand at some home rearing. This is nowadays a thing which anyone can do, given the equipment, a little time and a certain 'feel' for the job. Doing it on a small scale with rescued eggs may not produce the best results, as you have no way of telling how long the eggs were 'set' when you found them, but if you can get someone to learn how to do it, and perhaps save a few chicks in the process, the time may come when you decide to catch-up some pheasants, rear from the egg on a slightly larger scale and save yourself a good deal of money in the process.

Broody hens, if you can get them, make ideal mothers which produce chicks which are hardier, better developed and more able to fend for themselves than the best mechanically produced poults. Lightweight, crossbreeds make the best mothers, if you can get hold of them. Enquire of anyone with a few rough-living, garden hens or stackyard 'clockers' and ask them to save you any bird which goes broody. Ideally, it will be a bird in good health as diseases are easily transmitted and incubating drains a hen's vitality. Give the hen a dusting with an insecticide powder and settle it down on a clutch of dummy eggs.

The nest box should be large enough to allow the hen to move about without crushing the eggs, and should be sited in a partly sunny, partly shaded place. Make a comfortable, clean, dry and commodious nest and line it with hay. Feed the hen at the same time each day, give it time to defecate and stretch its legs, but be sure it returns to the eggs before they are chilled. The Game Conservancy has claimed that: 'More eggs are spoiled by the hen being allowed to stay too long off her eggs than from any other cause'. Handle the broody carefully, tether it to a stick at feeding time and keep the nest surrounds and the eggs damped with water, especially in an arid summer and at chipping time. The hen will look after the chicks, protect them, find them food and see to their welfare. You will provide chick crumbs and water and then a small run. Chicks which survive the first week or so will have a good chance of survival. A small patch of lawn with three cocks and three broodies (plus a spare in care of accidents) and fifteen eggs under each forms a very real contribution to the shoot, and holds the interest of the rearer through the summer months.

Alternatively, there are now many good, small domestic incubators on the market. Relatively cheap ones which can accommodate up to a hundred game bird eggs are about right for the small, domestic enterprise. Set the device at hatching status for the eggs that you find in threatened nests and you will be right for at least some of the time, and remember that each chick hatched from these clutches is a bonus. A paraffin brooder is ideal for protecting the chicks at night and during cold spells but an infra-red lamp on a long flex is cheaper and more foolproof for the small, back-lawn enterprise. Gradually harden off the chicks until, at four weeks or so depending on the weather, they will be independent of extra heat and will have two or three weeks to toughen themselves before being put out in the release pen.

Such brief notes are only intended to indicate the basic choice of methods which exist for the home rearer. Again, the Game Conservancy booklets *Incubation of Gamebird Eggs* and *Pheasant Brooder Rearing* have the last word on the subject. In my view, this series of papers for the practical gamekeeper is the best guide available and represents a major contribution to the whole sport of shooting. The booklets may be obtained individually from the Game Conservancy, Fordingbridge, Hampshire, or a complete set bound into a single book and called *The Complete Book of Game Conservation* is available and represents a sound investment.

An experienced keeper is a most useful ally when rearing chicks; he will advise you when you encounter problems and may even lend you a few coops and runs. For your first two seasons, when you are feeling your way with rearing, it is comforting to have a friendly expert who can bale you out of trouble. The expertise of the two professional keepers on our shoot has often proved invaluable. However, I would not discount the value of the amateur learning how to bring a coop of pheasants to maturity, even at the risk of a few losses. Too great a depth of expert knowledge in a few members deprives the keen but inexperienced ones of an interesting and rewarding experience. On our shoot, which depends upon bought-in poults, it is a touching scene when a member brings down a cardboard box containing the five pheasants he has managed to rear from two clutches of salvaged eggs. Each bird by then has become almost a family pet and it is with a conflict of strong emotions in which pride and regret are equally mixed that he releases them into a polyglot and

Steady dogs will be essential later on in the year. Now is the time to consolidate their training

anonymous batch of ours. One member on a shooting day rushed up indignantly waving a pheasant aloft. 'Look at this', he cried. 'Some so-and-so has gone and shot poor Arthur!' Few home-rearers will not be familiar with the feeling.

I make no excuse for emphasising how important it is that the guns should operate as a team. Each member will have his own responsibilities, but you are all striving to a common end and it is important that each should know the others as well as possible. The first shooting days are not the time for forming relationships, but for maintaining and enriching those already established. Strangers must be made to feel welcome and integrated with the rest as soon as possible. Early and late in the season, working parties will assemble to carry out the various chores which are necessary and the members will meet on those occasions, but mid-summer can be a slack time during which the shoot seems far away and you must try to redress the balance.

JUNE

One way of doing this is to have a series of light-hearted clay shoots, say weekly or fortnightly, on some part of the shoot where you will not be disturbing nesting game. A few clays is always a good way of rounding off a busy morning erecting or making your pens and hoppers, but to meet and shoot a score of 'birds' apiece on a Sunday morning is a valuable exercise in many ways. As well as pulling the members together, there is a chance to discuss details of shoot policy, to arrange future working parties and an opportunity for individuals to voice any minor problems or 'niggles'. Also you will be keeping shooting muscles in trim and ensuring that hand and eye have not lost their cunning. The event can be rounded off with a picnic and a bottle of beer or with a lunch at the local pub where the consolidation process can continue.

This is the season of clay shoots, and you might even consider forming a clay-shooting team to enter some local sporting shoots. You are not especially concerned with winning, but the experience of being a team member when opposed to other teams on a sporting occasion is one of the best makers of *esprit de corps* that I know.

I regard as a critical point in the formation of the Duke's Ground team a summer's day in our first season when we entered an East Anglian BFSS sporting shoot. The results are not relevant, but we were not disgraced and one of us won the Pool, but the experience of pulling together and being dependent upon one another was the best thing that could happen to the mixed bag of shooters who were thrown together with nothing more in common than a love of shooting. When the shooting season came round, much of the strangeness and awkwardness that might have clouded those first days just did not materialise.

In addition to clay shooting, June, being a slack month for the keeper without a chick-rearing programme, is a good time to be training the gun dog out on the grass meadow on the sunny days.

The summer keepering round is the chance to give the dogs a cooling swim, but keep them firmly to heel when in cover

7
July

Siting and setting up release pens – food – wild broods – trespassers – harvest

By July the farm crops are at their most lush state of growth, the corn is ripening and, by the end of the month, some of the winter barley will be harvested. With luck, your patches and strips of cover crops, the kale and maize, have also grown well and have the makings of the shelter and cover which will be so useful to your shooting later in the year.

While you will already have given the matter some thought, now is the time to come to the important decision about the siting of your mobile releasing runs. The portable sections, which I described in May and which one or more of your members will by now have completed, will be termed 'rearing pens' by the purist. In the strict sense, so they are but for our purposes this type of set-up is a release pen in all but name, and so I shall continue to describe it.

Depending on your acreage, you will wish to have more than one releasing point. The unkeepered shoot is vulnerable if all its birds are put down in one place and expected to survive with the small amount of attention you will be able to devote to them. We release in three widely separated places so that if disaster should strike one of them, all is not lost.

Do not choose places near the boundary. If you do so, your birds need only stray a little way and will be on a neighbour's land, a fact about which he might have few regrets. As a matter of principle you must draw your birds from the outside in and on shooting days drive them with the same idea. Pheasants are great wanderers and full-time keepers are for ever beating or 'dogging-in' their boundaries to keep their birds at home. In one instance, a pheasant was shot 13 miles from its home and even that is not exceptional.

Birds should be put down somewhere near a crop, a patch of your own cover or a wood which will provide an amenable habitat throughout the winter. If you set your pens in the corner of a cornfield, that corn will be cut, the stubble will possibly be burned and the field will be ploughed before September is out. The result is no shelter for the birds, so they will wander until they find some and your first efforts at holding them to a spot will have been frustrated. If there is a field of sugar beet handy, this is ideal as it is a crop which pheasants love, and in the Fen country it forms the basis for most of the game shooting which takes place. The birds will wander about in it and you can feed them there and they will be likely to stay.

It is not advisable to release your birds in places which are easily seen by passers by, such as in close proximity to public roads; even farm roads are best avoided. The sight of your wire pen sticking up in obvious view is an open invitation to people to go and have a look, even let the birds out by accident or design or perhaps steal them. Thefts from release and rearing pens have become more frequent in recent years. On the other hand, the pen must be reasonably convenient for service visits from authorised amateur keepers. It is no joke carrying sacks of food and 5-gallon cans of water to some obscure spot at the far end of a 50-acre field. The site should have a sunny aspect and be sheltered from the prevailing winds. It should be on fairly level ground and, ideally, should be on a spot where no pen stood last year. This consideration is a simple precaution against spreading diseases and, in the case of mobile pens, it is an easy one to take.

Careful thought is therefore needed before choosing releasing points which fulfil all these requirements. As the Fens are not noted for their trees, it is difficult on Duke's Ground to put down pheasants where they can learn to roost off the ground. On upland, wooded country this will be a thing to bear in mind but, as many of our pheasants roost or 'jug' on the ground, it is less important.

Let us assume that, like us, you have made two portable

releasing runs and have one established release pen. Assemble all your working guns on a Saturday or Sunday early in the month. If you are well organised, one day will suffice to get the job done. With luck, you will have chosen a sunny day when everything seems easier and jobs are done more quickly than when it pours with rain, but you will probably not be able to choose your weather. Arrange with the farm to borrow a tractor and a low, flat trailer; this should prove no problem as it will be a slack time on the farm, with no likelihood of weekend work. We are fortunate in that our gun who is a local farmer can always provide the required transport, while another member has a Land-Rover and trailer which is ideal.

Divide your team into three with the expertise and brute force divided evenly between them. Send the first team to the fixed release pen in the belt. You will find it carpeted with rank nettles and cow parsley, the pop-holes choked, wire sagging, some posts rotten at ground level and fallen branches collapsed on top of the wire. With a bill-hook, trim a clearing in the middle and other little patches here and there. Do not cut all weed growth as the poults will use overgrown areas as places in which to hide. Trim back trees which have grown to overhang the essential sunning area and remove dead or living branches which have fallen on the wire and which form bridges for vermin to get in or poults to get out. Make sure there is a strip of cleared ground around the whole perimeter both inside and outside the wire.

Next, check the wire carefully for holes. A stoat will gain entry through a surprisingly small chink and will hunt around persistently until he finds one. Mend these holes with fresh wire and, in the case of bad rust or a large rent, patch the place with a whole new section. Make sure the top edge of the wire is not sagging too loosely from the posts – climbing weeds such as old man's beard or bindweed will sometimes pull it down. A fairly loose top edge will make it harder for foxes and stray dogs to jump over so do not brace the top strand as taut as a violin string, but have it reasonably well braced all the same. Where staples have pulled out of the post they must be replaced, and where the post has rotted at ground level a new one must be inserted.

JULY

You will find that the pop-holes will have become choked with weeds and the wire 'wings' which guide the poults back in will have been bent over or lost. Clear out the apertures and re-set the 'wings' so that birds which are wandering round the outside will be subtly directed back into the safety of the run. Any old straw bales left from last year should be removed and burned, as they harbour diseases and fungoid growths. Use clean, fresh straw only. Set up feeders and water troughs, making sure that they have been sterilised, and leave your two dustbins with secure, tight lids ready for your corn and pellets. A supply of grit should be scattered on a patch of bare, dry earth which will serve as a dusting point later on. See that your sheet of corrugated iron, old door or other large piece of similar lumber is there in readiness to be a shelter from the rain. It is more economical of space to set this on four short posts than on straw bales. If you do decide to use posts, these can be established now whereas you will have to wait for bales until after harvest. Remember to set this roof at an angle so that the rain will run off. Finally, ensure that the gate or doorway to the enclosure shuts securely without any gaps at the bottom through which a predator may creep. If your pen is anywhere near a place where the public are likely to wander, you will need a padlock on the gate as a first-line deterrent to interference. This will need to be checked and oiled, and make sure that the keys are available and hidden in the usual place.

All this will take three keen men a good morning to do, and perhaps a part of the afternoon, especially if the pen is in a dilapidated state. When the work is completed, the pen will be ready to receive its complement of birds.

While all this is going on, the other two teams are busy putting up the portable runs. If you have done as I suggested, and assembled all the necessary components, accessories and tools a few weeks before, you will save everyone a good deal of wasted time hunting about for lost bits and pieces while your labour force stands idly by. If all is ready and the sets are colour-coded, the gear can be loaded onto the trailer and dropped off in the two places where it is required. Each set of equipment will have its assembly team in attendance.

It is simplicity itself to set up these pens, provided all the tools and the necessary pieces are to hand. Lay out the sections in a rectangular shape with two sections at each end. You do not want a long narrow pen but a short wide one which makes the best use of the ground. When the precise site has been established one helper should hold up one section in the place it is to go, while another digs the ground level so that the lower edge of the section is well embedded in the ground. Shovel away minor lumps and clods until the section is level. Drive in a wooden stake to support each end and set up the next section of the pen. Tie the stake and each end of the two sections together with orange baler twine. In this way, build up the pen, a section at a time, with a stake at each joint, until the whole thing is complete and rigid. Remember to include the section with the door at the point where you would normally approach the run.

Next, stretch the nylon netting over the top, slipping it over nails half-hammered in at regular intervals along the top. Make sure there are no gaps. A tall, T-shaped stick in the middle of the run will hold up the middle of the net and discourage dogs and foxes from jumping on top. The inside of the runs should be furnished with feeders and drinkers as in the fixed pen, but remember to use sparrow guards in order to train the birds to their future use. Cut some shady boughs – evergreen is best – and make a shelter in the shape of a wigwam in the middle of the pen. Any animal or bird kept in captivity should have a refuge into which to retreat and game birds are no exception. Put your sheet of corrugated iron onto its four stakes and all will be ready for the arrival of your birds.

It is a good idea to establish trapping points and a rat bait hopper somewhere near your pens. Any concentration of game birds will attract vermin and rats will arrive where there is corn. A Fenn trap in a tunnel should be set at two or three likely places round the run, but remember to make the entrance hole too small for a pheasant to squeeze in, otherwise one will surely do so. Set a fox snare round the foot of the run. A fox in your pen full of birds is an unmitigated disaster as it will more than likely kill the lot. While it is not often that a snare outside a release pen ever

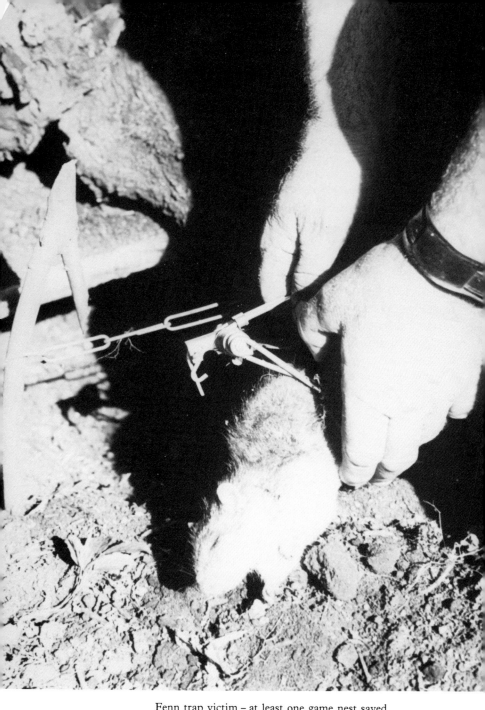

Fenn trap victim – at least one game nest saved

actually catches anything, its presence there will at least give the rearer peace of mind. Renardine, from Gilbertson and Page, an old patent fox repellent impregnated in string can be stretched round the run. Flashing road lamps, lanterns and scarecrows all have their keen supporters as fox deterrents; some people with a paranoia on the subject have even been know to try them all at once!

Food and grit may be delivered now. It is worth phoning your supplier to make sure that it is on its way. Some rearers use turkey pellets and claim a good rate of success. Pheasant pellets are rather more expensive, and cynics claim they are exactly the same as those which come in sacks with a picture of a turkey on the front! I am not a cynic in the matter, and, while I admit that poults can be successfully reared on turkey pellets, it is a mistake to take short cuts or to stint the poults at the feeding stage. The early period of any creature's growth is critical; cut down its food or give it poor quality and the results will seriously affect its future life.

When your food is delivered, store it at your headquarters in rat-proof containers away from the damp and leave some Warfarin sachets lying around. Nothing is worse than picking up a paper sack and having the contents pour out of the bottom through rat holes or damp patches.

This is also the month to be watching carefully for signs of wild broods which will now be more conspicuous than they were in June. Again it is the showery days which will have the birds creeping out of the corn to dry out on the roadways. Keep an eye open for roaming foxes and cubs of the year which will have large appetites and to which a brood of half-grown pheasants presents an attractive meal. Continue to walk the dyke banks looking at the earths and, if you find one occupied, deal with it straight away before the vixen has a chance to move the cubs which will by then be well-grown. Cymag gas in experienced hands or, preferably, a brace of terriers is the best sort of final solution.

High summer is the time when other people will be out in the countryside. A footpath through your shoot is a very mixed

Growing vegetation begins to provide safer cover and protection from prying eyes

blessing as are bramble patches thick with blackberries. People on a footpath have a right of way and may not be discouraged by you. However, if they have dogs which they encourage to rampage through the crops on either side of the path or if they stray from the straight and narrow you would do well to remonstrate. Some keepers shout, rave and threaten and talk of snares and deadly poisons which, they claim, pepper the surrounding fields. I do not agree with this approach – some of the walkers will be locals whom you will not wish to alienate but rather enlist as understanding allies. In any case, a soft, reasoned, but firm explanation of the damage that trespassers may unwittingly cause is more likely to be respected. Remember that, if it comes to the crunch, the law of trespass is sufficiently vague as not to give the landowner or shooting tenant the support he feels he deserves. Where there is loose stock, however, the situation is rather different, and domestic dogs must be kept on a lead. Any dog trespassing and doing proved damage, for example sheep worrying, is liable to be shot.

At the end of July some of the early corn will be cut. This is a busy time for the farmer and a period in which you must not trouble him with your problems. If you or any of the team has the time, an afternoon in the field with the combine is time well spent. You will have the time to chat with the man on the grain trailer, and this will be useful. If the men who work on the farm understand what you are trying to do, they can be potent allies, saving endangered nests, reporting concentrations of vermin and passing on other information which will be helpful to you. Have the gun and dog with you, as there is always the chance of a cornfield rabbit or even a fox. When the field reduces to the last few strips of uncut corn, broods of game birds will be seen running along the stubble in front of the combine. Like the modern silage cutter, the combine travels at trotting speed for a human, and broods of chicks can be easily swallowed by that great maw and lost for ever. A word with the driver to keep his eyes open is useful as he can easily slow down at critical moments and allow the birds to move off to safety. You can help by running the dog through the last few swathes as an early warning system.

The start of the harvest is also an important time for you as it will be your first real indication of how your wild stocks have survived the hatch. The corn is their principal cover and as it steadily diminishes you will see all revealed. Hens with one or two poults in tow are bad news, while large groups will fill you with optimism. The whole shooting policy for the coming winter will depend largely on what you see as the combines roar round.

8
August

Harvest – straw – ex-laying pen birds – tags and rings – releasing poults – feather-pecking – automatic feeders

In this month, the harvest is in full swing and by the end of it there ought not to be much corn left on the farm. Duke's Ground being on the Fen, the harvest is later than on higher ground, and we expect some corn to be standing as late as mid-September. The harvest jobs which you began in late July should be continued, following the combine, watching for late broods and mopping up the vermin. Stubble-burning, which was rife in the seventies, seems to have become less popular. This has been partly caused by the increased value of straw and tighter regulations by County Councils, but also by a greater appreciation of the risks by the farmers themselves. A quick burn is still a rapid way of destroying weed seeds and killing insect pests, but ravaged hedgerows, burned woods and even traffic accidents on smoke-covered roads have given farmers pause for reflection. As a shooter you are all in favour of restraint and like to see untouched stubbles left as long as possible with the seeds and insects spared to feed the birds. Anything you can do to persuade your farmer to adopt a non-burning policy should be done. He may not be fully aware that it is so opposed to the interests of young game birds.

It is likely that a good deal of the straw will be baled and either stacked on the farm or, increasingly often these days, sold in the field and taken away on huge lorries. So efficient has the baling/carting operation become that whole fields can be cleared completely in a single day. Straw is vital to the keeper. He needs it in his release pens, at his feeding points in winter, as windbreaks and even as seats in his beaters' waggon. You must bag some before it is too late, having first, of course, asked permission. This is likely to be forthcoming and you must organise a quick working party to collect half a trailer load of bales – about fifty or sixty – and take them to the shelter of your headquarters. Scatter a few Warfarin sachets behind them, otherwise they will become infested with rats. Those you need immediately for your release pens should be taken straight there and left in readiness.

By far the most important event of the month, and possibly of the whole year, is the arrival of your birds. You have shopped around to make your money stretch as far as possible and obtained your birds from sources investigated and secured earlier in the year. It is far too late to order any at this time of year, except in the event of a cancellation and if you are in the right place at the right time.

On Duke's Ground, we have adopted a policy of releasing a number of ex-laying pen birds. These are nearly all hens, but about 10 per cent cocks are usually included. Keepers have ambivalent views about these birds. Some release them with little expectation of them doing anything except fading away and dying. Others sell them to game dealers or butchers where they are sold as oven-ready birds over the counter. The rest sell them to the likes of us, secure in the belief that they are 'clapped-out' and virtually useless.

These birds were once semi-wild and, having survived the previous shooting season, probably possess powers of self-preservation denied to the majority of their cousins who filled the bag on shooting days. They are mature birds and, while they may be somewhat weary with egg-laying and bald where they have been regularly trodden, we have found them less likely to die for no apparent reason than poults. Those that have been heavily de-beaked are best avoided as they find it harder to fend for themselves in the wild, but any others will be useful to you. They will have been either brailed, that is, the flight feathers of one wing strapped down to prevent their flying off, or they will have been wing-clipped to the same end. The brails will have been removed, but in either case they are unable to fly well and while they are capable of evading a ground predator, providing they see it first, they have not the power to take to wing and vanish over the horizon as soon as you let them go.

The birds will arrive in travelling coops, preferably in the early evening. In hot weather they will be distressed after the journey and should be released into the pens as soon as possible after arrival. We put ours into two widely separated spots, as near the middle of good cover as we can manage.

If you decide to leg-ring or wing-tag your birds, this is the time to do it. This is a matter on which widely differing opinions are held. While it is understandable to wish to see how many of your released birds eventually end up in the bag, the actual exercise can prove a bitter disappointment. Some shoots make brave claims for their returns, but on unkeepered ground, ringing or tagging could prove traumatic. I have to own up to the fact that we have never dared to try it. We have the best intentions, and possess a new lot of 500 leg rings in two colours to distinguish the ex-laying pen birds from the poults, but we have stopped short of actually putting them on. There never seems to be time at the right moment and our hearts fail us at the prospect. This year we really mean to go ahead and use them, and prove once and for all just how effective our releasing programme is. The Stop Press news is that we did use rings; green for the poults and red for the ex-laying pen birds. Returns were poor (about 20 per cent), but we found out that the rings tend to come off, and we picked up a number in the release pen during the winter. However, we recovered some red-ringed pheasants, but no green, the second year after release, by which time they would have been at least three years old. Game Conservancy wing tags are only slightly more laborious to put on, but they do not fall off or become snagged. Check the bag carefully at the end of the day, recover the tags, and keep a meticulous record of the number you have retrieved.

With or without rings or tags, your ex-layers are quietly released into the pen. The less fuss and noise there is, the better so no more than two people will be present. Food and water will be there before the birds are put out, so that it is not necessary

Feeding the birds by hand; the best way, if you have time

for you to go blundering about topping up the hoppers and scaring the birds. The pheasants will be disorientated and nervous and the last thing you want is to have them piling up in a corner or crashing against the side-netting in panicky efforts to escape. Shut the door securely and retreat quietly, giving them the night in which to settle down and find their bearings and discover the food and water. They will probably need a good drink after the journey so see that a 5-gallon drinker is available and full to the top.

For food, use breeder pellets or maintenance pellets. Remember that the birds have suffered a taxing summer and they will need building up. It is likely that for the past few weeks they will have been fed on corn alone. If they are to be let out to face the winter in a strange place, their vitality will need improving. Find out what feeding call or whistle was used by their previous

Preparing to walk out and face the world

owner and use it on the two occasions a day when you go to feed. Feed generously – you have invested a good sum of money in these birds and skimping on their food is the falsest of economies.

Keep the birds in the pens for about two weeks depending on how soon they appear calm and contented. Keep an eye open for feather-pecking and bullying which might happen if you have put too many birds in too small a space. For a short period like this you ought to get away with it. At the end of the acclimatisation period, choose an evening of dry weather, feed as usual and untie the cord holding together the upright members of one end of the pen. If you then stand quietly at the opposite end, the birds will find the gap and file out in a quiet and orderly manner into the cover. When they have nearly all gone, move round and secure the pen, leaving five or six birds inside. Outside the pen you have established a feeding area comprising a hopper, a drinker, a broken, scattered straw bale and a good supply of food. Your object is to hold the birds nearby and to prevent them wandering off. Remember that they are in unfamiliar territory. All you can do is offer them a secure and well-fed habitat which will encourage them to stay.

The birds left in the run will call and help to keep the flock homing-in to the releasing area, and when you go down the following morning you will be likely to find a row of the released pheasants sitting on top of the run. Thereafter you can only maintain regular feeding, keep the area as undisturbed as possible and hope for the best. After another week, the remaining birds can be released and this will give you the chance to sterilise feeders and drinkers in the pen and put down clean straw ready for the arrival of your poults. It is not unusual for ex-laying pen birds to make a nest and begin to brood a clutch of eggs almost as soon as they are released. If any chicks hatch, they will be too backward to survive the winter, but at least you have ensured that the hen is anchored to the shoot and will not stray. We have found such nests within a few yards of the release pen.

The timing of this operation is important. Most keepers and game farms finish with their laying birds in July but, from your point of view, the later they are released on the shoot, the better. There is less corn in which they can escape, the shooting season is closer and the birds are less likely to wander away. Your supplier may insist on you receiving your stocks earlier, in which case you must make the best of it, but try to get him to keep them for as long as possible. From his point of view, they are superfluous once their usefulness has ended and they consume expensive food, so you may have to apply some diplomacy and a 'drink' to ease the problem.

The same applies to your poults which will arrive aged between six and ten weeks. Late releases usually provide better returns than early ones, and you are looking to put down your poults sometime at the beginning of this month. It is not really satisfactory to release them in the same pens as you used for your old birds, but as your enterprise operates on a financial shoestring, it is unlikely that you will have much choice in the matter. Take all precautions you can by cleaning all equipment. The really meticulous will move the runs to fresh ground, but this is time-consuming at a busy period and will not be easy to arrange. We have taken the, admittedly small, risk every year and have suffered no ill effects.

Introduce the poults into the runs just as you did the old birds. They should have been de-beaked to discourage feather-pecking and the ends of the primaries on one wing should have been cut off with scissors to prevent them flying blindly away or dashing themselves against the wire. Feed with poult pellets and after ten days of these begin to mix clean wheat in with it, so that by the time they are released they are all but weaned onto corn which will be their staple diet thereafter. It is likely that you may be guilty of some slight overcrowding and again you must watch closely for signs of feather-pecking. Providing plenty of greenstuff in the run or hanging corn cobs on strings from the roof will help prevent them from becoming bored. Pheasants are extremely cruel to each other and will quickly gang-up on a weakling or one which has already been attacked and is showing blood. They will harry it here and there, giving it no rest until it dies.

We keep an 'Emergency Ward Ten' for any casualties identified before they have suffered too much damage. This is a small coop and run where about six birds can be kept in peace and quiet – in the hope that some of them at least will recover. If left in the main run, they would certainly die, so at least you are giving them a chance.

It is important to feed at the same times each day. Any experienced keeper will tell you that he only has to be an hour late to his feed ride in the morning and half his birds will have wandered off having become tired of waiting. If, as is possible, you have a rota of feeders, they will be more likely to arrive at

Ex-laying birds can be released on the shoot, and may nest in the same year

disparate times of their own convenience and the birds will never develop a systematic feeding pattern and a time at which they will turn up expecting food. Be firm with your feeders and insist on precise timing or hand the task over to one or two who can provide a regular service.

An excellent aid to the do-it-yourself keeper is one of the automatic feeders which have been developed during the past twenty years. The principle is simple enough. A large hopper made of glass-fibre or galvanised metal holds the food. A spinning device, similar to a granulated fertiliser distributor, is on the base; a siren, a time-clock and a heavy-duty battery complete the set. The clock can be set for a number of times a day at which the siren will sound and the spinner will shoot out a spray of corn or pellets for a regulated period of time. Basic Pavlovian animal psychology soon causes the birds to respond to the stimulus of the sound which they will quickly link with the distribution of food. It is quite startling to see the birds respond by running and flying in from considerable distances as soon as the siren begins to sound. These devices seem expensive when one considers the price of the components, but they give good value on the unkeepered shoot and can be used well into the season. Some call them the lazy keeper's friend. Your team will not be lazy keepers, but they will be keepers with many demands on their time.

There are several types of automatic feeder, notably the one made by Parsons of Nailsea which runs on the principles described. Some are operated by highly sophisticated 'chip' technology. As a refinement, a collar can be fitted to the spinner, which means that the food is flung out at an angle. This is useful where you might need to scatter the feed from the bank and into a pond to feed wildfowl. A good feeder will take corn with straw and chaff mixed up with it which would choke the more traditional type. Details of automatic feeders are given in Appendix 4.

When the poults have become acclimatised and seem to be growing too big for their little area, they should be released in three or four big batches, fed heavily round the run and left in peace. You will see little groups of them away from the feeding area and your dog may gently chivvy them back 'home'.

Even with the automatic feeder, you must keep an eye on your birds. Any keeper of livestock knows the value of standing quietly and watching his charges. In that way he will note the halt and the lame and be able to assess the general health and morale of the group. A general gamebird wormer should be introduced in the water and, while outbreaks of gapes will be less likely than they would on ground with is used year after year for rearing, watch out for 'snicking' and treat any such symptoms with Gapex, available from Gilbertson and Page. For all problems concerning rearing and medicaments, the Game Conservancy booklets will usually have the answer.

9
September

Duck – corn – beaters – dog-men – insurance – shooting dates – driving – food and water

The first day of September is the official opening of the shooting season for partridge and duck, but the small shoot organiser will not start shooting yet, unless he is lucky enough to have a lead-in of mallard onto a stubble or resting on a dyke or pond on the shoot. In either case, the season may be christened with a flight or two. These duck are a temporary, fleeting harvest and may fairly be taken advantage of while they remain with you. If you have water, a real blessing on any shoot, some duck will return in the cold weather and bring others with them.

Much of your keepering time this month will be spent consolidating your work of the previous weeks, looking after your released birds, collecting straw and building up a store of grain for feeding, enough to last until the end of the following March. All shoot members should collect as much as they can from their various sources, and bring it to your headquarters where you will store it in rat-proof, waterproof, 40-gallon drums. Continue to collect odd bales of straw which have fallen off trailers or been left lying around. The harvest will be drawing to an end and foxes will now have ceased to be a threat to you, but the key position tunnel traps will still be picking up the occasional stoat or rat.

This is now the time for some key planning as you are approaching the time of your first organised shoots, those days to which the previous months' preparation, labour, expense, anxiety and many hours' work have all been directed. First, you must see to it that a team of beaters is established. The more

Each gun will provide at least one beater. They need to be welded into a team

regular this team can be, the better and a team of beaters which comes to know the shoot, the lie of the land and the likely behaviour of the birds is worth its weight in gold. Money is short, and paying out a fiver a head for fifteen beaters every time you shoot is going to increase the bill by an enormous amount. Spending money unnecessarily is not one of your briefs. At Duke's Ground we have developed the firm rule that each gun provides one or more beaters per shoot. Mostly they will come for the fun of it, but their gun might provide them with lunch and the shoot can lay on a drink at lunchtime. As time passed and we felt a lack of dogs in the field, it was suggested that each gun should provide a beater with a dog. Guns entered the search with enthusiasm and we were lucky, after a very few weeks, to be able to field a team of dogs and beaters of all ages and both sexes which I would back against any in East Anglia.

It is no good asking guns to find such beaters a week before the shoot. A good month is necessary to make sure that the right people are found. Small sons and wives who only want a day's vigorous walking are always welcome, but the experienced man or woman with a controllable, hunting/flushing dog is a key figure and bag-filler on the shoot. In time you may feel able to appoint a head beater, someone who can take charge of the team, issue instructions, control the line and maintain morale. Someone who shows the necessary qualities will eventually emerge and in time could be allowed to carry a gun in certain cases or be rewarded in some other way. Pickers-up should be found on the same system. Good ones are in great demand, and their services can command high fees, so it might be necessary to pay two for your shoot, unless you have some close friends who would turn out in return for a brace of pheasants and a lunch.

Having made sure that this important matter is well in hand, another essential is to see that all guns carry third party insurance. While an accident is always a disaster, if it results in insurance claims which by their huge size are unpayable you are guilty of an avoidable evil. Membership of BFSS and BASC ought to be a condition of membership of the shoot – every sportsman ought to contribute towards the protection and furtherance of his sport. Full membership of BASC includes third party insurance for sporting accidents up to a value of half a million pounds. See that every gun is so covered, and also guests. As an alternative, but less satisfactory arrangement, a group scheme may be adopted.

Another important decision to be taken in the early part of this month is to establish your shooting dates. It may be that the terms of your lease will limit the number of shoots you may hold but you must still decide when they will be. It is impossible to suggest rules as each shoot will make its own. On a tiny place of a few acres which you are building up from scratch, you might be able to afford only one or two days in your first season, whereas a good arable or mixed farm of a thousand acres or more might be able to accommodate ten full days. The vital factor to consider is the so-called 'shootable surplus' on which all your plans will depend. Once the ground is properly stocked, only those birds extra to that number may be shot; to over-shoot would be to erode stocks and jeopardise the future. The size of the shootable surplus depends on the success of the breeding season which, in turn, depends on a combination of good weather and your efforts as an amateur keeper. After a wet, cold summer on a farm where crows and foxes have been allowed to breed freely, the shootable surplus may well be nil; it may even be that breeding stocks will have been eroded.

Your influence in controlling vermin, feeding the pheasants, providing cover and artificially building up the population by releasing reared birds is instrumental in increasing the shootable surplus. The more you can do in these respects, the more you will have to shoot at in the winter. This is your greatest incentive to do as thorough a job as your time will allow. By September you should have a rough idea of the size of the population of shootable birds and you will know how many days you will be able to shoot. There is a temptation to overdo it and slip in just one extra day, especially if you feel that some guns may not have had much sport, but this must be resisted. A little restraint and an awareness of the necessity of conserving stocks will pay dividends in the years to come.

Whether you shoot on Saturdays or weekdays is simply a matter of mutual agreement. That decision will have been made before you invited the guns to join. Those who work during the week will obviously find a Saturday more convenient and it is easier to get beaters, especially schoolboys, on that day. Even so, a surprising number of shoots operate on weekdays.

If you have any partridges, you ought to try for them in mid-October. By then the covies will be strong on the wing. While you will not be driving your pheasants, one or two will come over the guns and fully mature ones, flying well, ought to be shot. It is not likely that you will make a large bag of partridge and the odd pheasant or 'various' will make up the tally. There will be stubbles and lightly cultivated ground and the fields of roots, if you have any, will still be there. Some potatoes will have been lifted and this crop, with its weeds and the shelter of its

Picker-up in action on the stubble

ridges is excellent holding for partridges. In mid-October, there should still be enough left for you. This day will also bring to light any problems of management on the shooting day and there will still be time to iron them out before your pheasant days.

Your big days will start in mid-November and go through until Christmas. They may be fortnightly or three-weekly depending on stocks and the state of the crops. Too much cover is as bad as too little and your best days will occur when root fields, such as sugar beet, are half-harvested. This means an important meeting with the farmer, and while he will be unable to predict the precise state of the crops three months hence, he will have a rough idea of what he will have left. Even then, excesses of the weather and market fluctuations can cause his calculations to go adrift. You will aim to leave your strips and corners of game cover until after the farm crops have gone. After Christmas you will arrange one or possibly two potters round the boundary in search of the old cock birds which have eluded you all season. Quite possibly you will decide to leave the hens after the second shoot; this will depend on the stock of birds you are carrying.

Thus, deciding on shooting days is far more than simply sticking a pin in the calendar. Once the days have been arranged, circulate all members with a printed list with place and time of meeting and the type of day, eg Full pheasant, Cocks only and so on. The sooner you can do this the better, so that members can make their arrangements well in advance and avoid double-bookings.

Once that is done, you must start to think about what form the various drives will take. You are looking for quality shooting and maintaining your policy of not turning the place into a glorified rough shoot. This was in your mind when you started out, and while you might not be able to show the quantity of birds seen on an established, keepered shoot, there is no reason why you should not emulate them in standards of organisation and the quality of the birds you present.

Both pheasants and partridges will fly in the direction they want to go and no amount of flag waving will make them deviate more than a little. Home to them is where they were reared or where they were fed, while partridges prefer to fly to fields with which they are familiar. Pheasants will usually be flushed from cover, either a farm crop, a wood or one of your specially planted areas. This means that each pheasant drive will end in a piece of cover or the whole drive might consist of driving the cover alone.

On a keepered shoot where the birds have been 'fed-in' on the morning of the shoot and kept in with stops until the shooting party arrives, the problems are few. You, however, are dealing with a high percentage of wild birds which will be scattered and which need to be moved into the cover from open ground or along dykes and hedgerows. Therefore you will be looking at your areas of cover, assessing which way the birds will fly and where the standing guns will be positioned. Then you cast your eyes far in the opposite direction to see where the beaters will start. This place must have access for a tractor or Land-Rover with a trailer, even in wet or snowy weather. If you are able to

At the start of the day, drawing for position is fair to all

muster about fifteen beaters plus two walking guns, you will need to deploy them in a line in which they are not too far apart, otherwise they will 'walk over' game which will lie doggo or even dodge back between them. In dense sugar beet or kale, beaters should ideally be close enough together to be able to hold hands. This might be possible in your strips or when the root crop has been reduced to the last few rows, but on open ground they may be twenty or more yards apart. Envisage them spread out along the starting line; those with dogs will bring in the hedges and ditches or other rough places.

Sometimes a likely hedge or ditch will run into the proposed drive at an angle or there might be a stubble just off the line which you would like to include. Splinter groups of beaters or reliable dog-men will be deputed to bring in these pieces. Game will move quietly forward in front of them until it arrives at the cover whence it will be flushed.

By walking round and using your map of the farm, you will be able to devise a number of drives. With experience you will change some of them, perhaps even reverse them if you find that the birds have a line to which they remain faithful. Duke's Ground has just such a place which is in the form of a river bank, right on the boundary. We tried to drive away from this and into the middle of the farm but, no matter what we did, they flew back to it. In the end we had to concede and put guns at the foot of the bank. We still drove it the other way, but had the guns behind the beaters with only a couple of lone scouts out in front. Eventually, if you are shooting woods, scrubland or other permanent cover, you will evolve the best system of driving which will work year after year. With ordinary farm crops which change annually, you will have to adjust the drives accordingly, but even then you will find that certain places are more attractive and hospitable to game than others.

A common fault with small, amateur-keepered shoots is that they tend to drive only the best places and leave large tracts of farmland untouched. Even a professional keeper will slip in the occasional rather unproductive drive once or twice in a day, if only to husband his stocks. It is easy to become caught up in the treadmill of wanting to show clouds of birds every drive. To make the most economic use of your land you should use it all; after all, you are paying rent on it, and you ought to bring in those great tracts of plough which you feel to be barren. I remember a shoot which I ran for a number of years in Norfolk, where all our shooting was concentrated on the shelter belts and other cover. We had a hare shoot in late February when vast areas of heavy plough and cultivated land which we had not driven in the season were brought in. I was amazed at the game which lay on this apparently bleak and untenanted ground. Partridge, pheasant and even duck came pouring over in a way which would have made the best game drive of the year. The lesson is that game birds are not stupid, and having been driven and shot at they will quickly discover the places where there is peace and quiet.

You must divide all your shoot into drives; on a small acreage you may have little choice. A mixed day will include some open

Shoot captains must give clear directions. Half-way through a drive is too late

country as well as some cover, and discerning guns will appreciate what you are trying to do. Late in the season it may be that you are left with only your home-planted cover crops, but, like a good poker player, do not be tempted to show your hand too soon and all at once.

You have chosen your dates and conceived your drives. There will be plenty of food for birds – insects, stubbles and weedy patches will be larders for them – but it is wise to maintain your regular feeding points, especially at the releasing areas. Your released birds will still be haunting those places and they must become accustomed to finding food there. If you feed with a mixture of corn and pellets, the pheasants will find this more attractive than corn alone and be more likely to remain. Dusting spots may be established in the lee on the sunny side of a hedge, and a tin sheet set over each to keep it dry. September being a dry month means that birds will be thirsty. Use your big drinkers or polythene sheeting laid in a dug or natural depression in the ground. In the Fens with their maze of dykes, drains and rivers, watering game birds is not a problem.

The end of the month marks the beginning of shooting proper, and the keepering tasks which have kept you busy since February are drawing to a close. Now you will see how effective it has all been.

10
October

Working party for pens – the first shoot – partridge driving – flags – portable butts – transport – pegs – lunch – acorns – potato harvest – game diary and vermin book

October will see the farm cropping and layout taking the shape which it will assume for most of the shooting season. There will be stubbles, some ploughed land, some ground with the surface broken by a chisel plough (good for partridges) and fields of root crops still untouched. You have convinced the farmer that he might as well leave you some stubbles, especially those which are strategically placed for your cover crops and your releasing points. The lush vegetation on the verges and dyke-sides will look overblown and already past its best. The heavy dews of the early mornings will be upon it and the first frosts will make it droop, go brown and die. On an intensively farmed shoot, these forgotten clumps are all capable of holding a bird or two and the farmer who is overkeen on keeping up appearances and who sprays or mows these places is not acting in the best interests of his game stocks.

A job for the early part of this month is to gather in all your rearing equipment and store it safely at headquarters. It is easy to leave a jumble of pen sections leaning against a hedge where they became soaked through and begin to deteriorate and we have been guilty of this, but it means more work the following spring when you come to prepare for the next rearing season. A small working party with a tractor and trailer can do the job and make your equipment snug and dry for the winter. The feeding areas, sparrow-guard hoppers, broken straw and watering points will remain on the sites of the releasing areas and your birds will still be using them.

In the middle of the month takes place that great event, your first shooting day. You will have walked and driven round the shoot as often as possible in the early autumn and you should know the fields on which the covies feed and where they shelter. You will combine this information with the half-formulated driving plans which you made last month and will work out eight, good, long drives with a ninth as a reserve. Eight is the traditional number of drives for a driven shooting day and long practice has shown that it is a reasonable number, but there is no reason why you should not deviate from this as circumstances might dictate. For partridge shooting you will not be concerned with driving any cover and you should keep well away from your pheasant concentrations.

The principle of partridge driving is to drive from stubble to roots and out again. Consideration must be given to natural flight lines and to the wind direction on the day. A partridge will not fly far into a stiff head wind before it swings away and out over the flank. Make your plans in such a way that it is not a major task to reorganise the drives on the day. Beaters will need to be armed with flags and may be quite far apart, with dogs at heel, as partridges are usually easy to flush. Sometimes, especially in wet weather, a large covey will play hide and seek with you in the roots in which case some dog work is called for. Flags, which used to be made of white linen, are now made of sections of white, polythene fertiliser bags which can be tacked onto the end of a stout stick. When waved in a certain way these flags make a satisfying whipcrack noise which increases their effectiveness. The distant sight and sound of these flags will start the birds moving early, and a key man on the flank can, by timely use of his, turn a covey back into the drive which would otherwise have been lost. Old-time partridge keepers were masters at managing teams of beaters with flags but the art has almost died out and it was a long-acquired skill.

You might also consider making portable butts. Partridge do not care to fly over human figures standing in the open, so butts cut in the hedges or made of straw bales are employed on proper partridge shoots. Unless you have belts of trees or tall hedges

Briefing the beaters – make sure they understand exactly what you want

over which to drive the birds you will find yourselves at a disadvantage. On your shoot with its few partridges, it is not worth the trouble of making permanent butts, so lightweight portable ones will be useful and might make all the difference to the way the birds behave and hence to the bag. These can be made out of two bamboo canes, 6ft 6in long with a sheet of hessian or scrim netting 4ft deep and about 5ft long tied or tacked on to them. It will look rather like a marching banner. The whole thing can be rolled up round the two sticks and handed to a gun as he goes to his place. When he arrives there, he simply unrolls the hide, jabs the ends of the sticks in the ground until he can just see over the top of the hessian and there he is. An approaching partridge will see nothing to cause it alarm and it ought to fly straight over and provide a chance. At the end of the drive, the gun picks up the hide, rolls it neatly and returns with it to the trailer. In this way, eight portable hides will last for a whole day's shooting, cost little to make and, with care, will last for a number of seasons.

Appoint a head beater and a senior gun, and spend an evening with them discussing the drives you have chosen. It looks unprofessional if, on the day, you stand round trying to make others understand what you want to do. I have seen these exercises in non-communication happen quite often, and at the end of them people tend to know rather less than they did before. A quiet instruction, 'beaters this way' or 'guns follow me' instils confidence and saves time.

The discussion will establish the order of drives so that one follows logically from another and travelling time is cut to a minimum. You will need to decide when to take lunch, and organise the logistics of the transport. You are short of both helpers and finance so that you will have to economise. Rather than pay a tractor driver, for example, one of the guns could take the beaters to their starting point, drop them off and drive back and take his place with the guns. This saves a man and means that the trailer is waiting in the right place at the end of the drive. Unless your shoot is very compact, transport of some sort is a necessary evil and on our place we cannot manage with less than two vehicles. You will have to arrange to borrow tractors and trailers or some of your guns will be able to help. Our farmer member has a Land-Rover horse-box and this is ideal, better in many ways than a farm trailer. It keeps out the wind and rain, is roomy and, with a line of straw bales round the side, is comfortable. Ours is one of the blessings of our shoot.

Our latest acquisition has been a walk-in builders' van with bench seats. It cost less than £100; it was resprayed a discreet Lincoln Green, and now serves ideally to transport the guns and their dogs. It is neither taxed nor insured but travels only on private farm roads, and is parked in the cart shed at headquarters. One mechanically-minded member of the team is in charge of this vehicle, services it and starts it on cold shooting mornings.

We decided to peg the drives for all our shoots in the approved

Pegs may, for the do-it-yourself man, be discarded

fashion, but abandoned the idea before we had even started. First, it took much longer to put them out than we had imagined and the time could be better spent doing other things, and, secondly, changing conditions meant altering the gun placings each time. While it appears more casual than you might like, it is easier and more adaptable to place your guns individually, covering all the necessary places. It might be possible to peg a wood or other area of permanent cover, stock and farming operations permitting, but we dispensed with it. We never entertain more than two guests at any shoot and the old hands who know the drives can see that everyone ends up in the right place. Having no pegs does not mean that you do not draw for position. To do otherwise would be as unfair as it would be confusing. Draw for numbers in the usual way, and advance two each drive, and the shooting should be evenly spread amongst you.

Arrangements for lunch should be made. Here again there is

great variety of practice among different shoots. Some shoot all day, breaking only for the briefest snack, and eat a substantial meal at tea-time. This makes sense especially on short winter days when you can easily waste the best hour of the day sitting in a shed eating sandwiches. We will look at the eating arrangements again when it comes to pheasant shooting, but in October with its long, golden evenings, there is no such pressure on time and a mid-day break will be appreciated, especially by dogs and humans who have allowed themselves to get out of condition during the summer. For this occasion guns and beaters should bring a packed lunch, but the shoot funds will have to provide the drinks. We run a small, weekly kitty from which our efficient bar steward is able to keep our portable bar (a large wooden box) well stocked. This too must be put in hand well before the shoot day. The place in which you have your lunch should contain some rudimentary furniture so that people can sit down. Straw bales can be used but benches and trestle tables are much better. Again, these arrangements must be put in hand before the day.

The more one does in helping to organise a shoot, the more it seems that one is concerned with peripheral details of this nature and less with actually firing the gun or bagging pheasants. However, these other matters must be attended to if members and guests are to have an enjoyable day. There is no reason why you should not seek to do things the right way with as much style as your limited resources can muster. You might, for example, have to consider car parking, recalling that you might have to find room for twenty cars. If there is a large concreted farmyard available, fine, but what if there is not and the fields are saturated after a week of heavy rain?

Other items you will need to bring include money to pay those helpers who have not been brought by guns, position finders to draw for places, a whistle, a horn to start and end drives, a knife, string already cut into short lengths ready to hang up any birds you may shoot; all this, together with your own personal shooting paraphernalia, will have to be remembered. It is worth making a check list and ticking off the items and jobs as they are done. It might read something like this:

Planks over dykes help the day run smoothly, but ask the farmer's permission before positioning them

Arrange drives	Lunch arrangements
Brief head beater and senior gun	Drink – collect subs
Transport and drivers	Brief pub for evening
Flags	Position finders
Portable butts	Whistle
Car park	Horn
Sweepstake	Game cards
Strings	Prepare briefing for guns – safety, etc
Outlet for spare game (a little optimism does no harm!)	
Own shooting equipment, dog etc	

By the time the day has arrived and everyone is moving off for the first drive, you are justified if you feel relieved, but even then your worries are not over. Birds go astray; the head beater shows that he misunderstood an instruction which you had thought crystal clear. A guest is waving his gun around in a lively manner. Why have the beaters started before the last gun is in position? How could Jim miss an easy covey like that? Whose is that dog out of control in the roots? Where are the birds? These are just a few of the thoughts that might assail you, if you are the worrying kind. By that time it is too late to change very much, and you would be best advised to stop worrying and enjoy yourself. The drive has been set in motion and while you might learn some lessons for next time, there is no point in trying to put things right there and then. Have a pleasant day, but make a mental note of what goes wrong and the areas which need tightening up.

Captain for the day is a role which ought to be shared among the guns. They will soon find that it involves more than exuding general bonhomie. As well as conducting and directing the various drives, the captain must see that everyone is happy and encouraged, that guests are made to feel welcome, that high standards of safety are observed, that game is distributed and that any little unexpected problem is quickly solved in a quiet and cheerful manner.

So much for the first shooting day, a high spot in your calendar. We will meet the gentle art again later in the season on the pheasant shoots, but this much information, when applied or adapted to your own local conditions, should be enough to see you through your first day. Each time thereafter will be more familiar and therefore easier until you eventually evolve your own ways of doing things.

Things to look for at the end of October include the possibility of a bumper acorn or beech mast crop. The former is especially relished by pheasants and they will wander a long way to find them. On Duke's Ground we have a single row of old oak trees and it is uncanny how quickly the pheasants find the acorns. It was not unusual to see a score or more at any time of day, pecking about and waiting, it seems, for the next acorn to fall. If you have no oak trees and your neighbour has many, bad luck. You may have to continually 'dog in' that boundary to hold your birds and feed your own cover generously. If all your members spend a morning collecting acorns and are able to produce a sackful each, these may be mixed with your regular feed to make

Picker-up and back gun

an attractive draw. They have the advantage over corn that they are not so easily stolen by rats, mice and small birds.

Before the potatoes are harvested, it has become customary to spray off the tops with a dilute acid so that they do not impede the onward rush of the harvester. This is a ghastly practice for late broods of game birds and the potato harvest usually starts in September when young poults are still in the roots. You have only to walk through recently sprayed potatoes to see your trouser legs and even boots gradually disintegrating. The effect on birds can be imagined and this is a great cause of mortality anywhere that potatoes are grown. The best you can do to ease the problem is to liaise closely with the farmer and dog out the fields before he sprays, but even then birds are likely to come creeping back at night. It is most frustrating to lose birds in this way, especially when you have been protecting them all year, and it represents a classic example of shooting and farming interests coming into conflict.

Game cover – here sunflowers and kale – is essential in the Fens

By the end of the month you will have your first shoot behind you and you will have a good idea of the size of the shootable surplus. Your remaining shoot days are planned and there is little more for you to do. Start a detailed game diary and carefully record everything that is shot, even the sexes of pheasants, and some notes on how the drives went. Some amateur keepers have a vermin book which records how and where predators were killed. Both books will be useful in the future, as patterns of behaviour have a habit of repeating themselves and to rely only on your memory is to place your trust in a fallible instrument.

11
November

Feed corn – conservation – the pheasant day – the shoot supper – handling game – game card – guests – safety

The first frosts will be killing off the vegetation, and a few fields of roots, your sown game cover, woods and spinneys and perhaps one or two stubbles will be the only covering on the land. The rest of the farm will be ploughed land and if the autumn is mild, some drilling of winter corn will have already taken place. Natural food for game birds will grow less by the week – every frost and each acre ploughed takes its toll of insects and seeds. The result should be that pheasants begin to draw in to your feed areas in the shelter belts and strips of cover. Some will never have strayed far, but those that have wandered will half remember and come back home. We tried a ploy to show the movement of our pheasants by putting down some pure white poults at each release point. These conspicuous markers acted as indicators of straying patterns; they showed clearly on our black Fen soil and could be seen a long way off. If these still crop up round the feeding areas in late autumn, it suggests that you may be holding a number of your reared birds. At the time of writing, mid-March, I have just returned from doing some chores on Duke's Ground where I saw a pure white, mature hen bird out feeding in the evening sun with her more soberly dressed sisters. This was within two fields of where we released two white birds last July. When I stopped to gloat over the sight, she 'clapped' down on soil as black as soot in the fond hope that this would make her invisible. White birds are also conspicuous to poachers and predators, but they have their uses.

Birds making their way into cover means that the feeding must be stepped up and this must be continued until the end of the following March. Pheasants will not need to find empty hoppers very often for them to wander away in search of a more regular food supply. You will still be feverishly collecting corn and bagging straw bales to keep this programme going. Grain is all harvested but it is being moved from bin to bin, dressed in barns, sold in lorry loads or put into sacks. Each of these operations will result in a small amount of wasted grain, unthreshed ears and sweepings which will be either thrown away or fed to the hens. You know what to do! If you run short, you will have no alternative but to buy some as a feeding programme is one of the three main props of your shooting. With wheat retailing at the moment at about £100 per ton, it will erode your hard-won funds if you have to buy very much. Anyone who moves on the fringe of agricultural circles should be able to obtain a few sacks of some sort of grain and if all ten of you do this you will accumulate enough to see you through, provided you do not waste it and feed it to sparrows. Feeding birds in cover will be one of your regular winter keepering tasks.

However, it is shooting which takes precedence from mid-November up to Christmas and your pheasant days will show just what improvements your team has been able to make since you took over your run-down and underpopulated patch of ground the February before. In the first season or after a poor breeding year, you will be concerned with conservation and will not worry about the amount of sport you have. Some guns may not sympathise, especially if they see what appear to be some encouraging populations of birds feeding on the stubbles. Those doing the keepering will know better how many birds per acre you can muster and are not deceived by apparently large congregations. Those guns who are interested only in firing their pieces and in the size of the bag are not really the sort you want in your team. You prefer those who take you quietly aside and say you are shooting too many hens or suggest you cancel the next shoot as the birds seem to be getting scarce. We shot barely a dozen hens during the first season on Duke's Ground, knowing that we were shooting for a future. The result was a much better season

Flanking guns are important on all drives, especially in wild country with no established flight paths

the following year and a higher shootable surplus.

Any year, at any time, you ought to feel free to call a halt to hen shooting, even half-way through a day. Each hen killed might lay a dozen eggs and produce five more pheasants for you next year. Thus, each season and even each day must be seen in the context of the quality of the breeding/releasing cycle and the number of birds you are killing. A team of brilliant shots, for example, would be able to mop up your shootable surplus in half a day. Will Garfit who runs the do-it-yourself man's dream of a small shoot in Cambridgeshire has adopted an interesting releasing system which obviates all need for difficult decisions about what you ought to shoot. He releases all cocks and shoots not a single hen throughout the season. This means that only the released cocks and a few wild ones are shot, while the hens on which the future depends, are all spared. His ground is suited to shooting a high proportion of his released birds, but the scheme sounds attractive. Its long-term effects have yet to be felt but Will is optimistic that the wild stocks will improve. I commend the idea for examination by other amateur keepers. A slight problem for us is that buying our poults 'on the cheap' we cannot be particular about the balance of the sexes, although in more mature, easily sexed, birds, cocks are cheaper.

The general arrangements for your 'big' pheasant days will be similar to those for your mixed partridge and cocks day. Drives, beaters, pickers-up, transport and so on will all be organised in the same sort of way. The white flags may be dispensed with unless you intend to slip in a partridge drive during the day or you may decide to issue a trusted flanker with one; he may be able to turn a bird or two your way in the course of the day. Remember to use farm root crops at this time of year and also some apparently less productive areas, saving your own cover and the woods until after the crops have gone. You are seeking to eke out your stocks for as long as possible.

Organise everything much as you did for the partridge day last month and benefit from the lessons you learned then. The nights will be drawing in and before long there will not be much shooting for you after 4pm. This is the time to reconsider your lunch arrangements and to ask yourselves whether you can afford to lose the best hour of the day. The answer might well be that you can, especially if you have few birds and are worried about being able to offer enough reasonable drives. In this case, a leisurely day will suit you perfectly, and the partridge day type of packed lunch in the headquarters will be satisfactory. However, if a bag is there for the making, there is much to be said for pushing on and finishing early. It is a disaster to drive roosting cover or kale while there is barely enough light by which to shoot. The birds may come out well enough, but where they finish their flight and whether they return is a matter of doubt. Good cover, especially kale, should never be driven late in the day but should be dealt with early on. Far better finish the day when there is light in the sky and avoid the urge to 'get in a quick one'. How rarely is such a rushed, last-minute effort a success.

Beaters and flanking guns, cementing relationships between drives

If you decide to have your main meal after the shoot, the local pub might be pressed into service. So many pubs now serve good, homely food that you should be able to find a suitable one within easy reach. The licensing laws of the land are such that the doors are closed to you until 6pm and you are faced with having to kill two hours between 4 and 6pm. You may sit around the headquarters in the gathering gloom and rising wind and make use of the portable bar, but this quickly palls and people tend to drift off home. The answer is to get the landlord to apply for a series of occasional licences on your behalf. Give him a list of your shooting dates and, for less than a fiver for them all, the necessary formalities can be completed. The result is that all of you, youngsters included, may remove to the hostelry at about 4.30pm, take advantage of a roaring fire and order some food. This keeps shooters, guests, beaters, wives and dog-men together and preserves the bonhomie and corporate spirit of a shoot. To

The do-it-yourself shoot cannot operate without the support of wives and girlfriends

me, this is a very important aspect of any shoot, and a shoot where everyone rushes home as quickly as they can is a poor sort of place which takes its pleasures sadly.

The plan we intend to adopt next year is even better. The wives of two of the guns have generously offered to cook and serve a hot three-course meal after the shoot in the farm centre, a modern, heated building used on weekdays by farm workers for their lunch breaks. It is already furnished with chairs and tables and, with a heated food trolley provided by the ladies, guns and beaters can be catered for. This sort of arrangement is probably the best of all: not everyone cares to go to the pub and pay its prices. The food can be produced at cost by enterprising ladies and the portable bar is always on hand for the thirsty.

Having dealt with that important matter, the midday break remains. On Duke's Ground Shoot, we are fortunate in that the wife and daughter of one of the guns arrive at a pre-arranged time with a sort of makeshift field kitchen serving hot soup and baked potatoes and butter. This is excellent, being warming, quick to serve and eat and a good deal more appetising than a packet of cold cheese sandwiches. I hope that your shoot will find itself as fortunately placed.

The handling and distribution of the game is another matter which will concern you as the bags begin to build up. Treat dead game carefully and do not allow it to become dirty or spoiled in the wells of Land-Rovers where it is jumbled by dogs and muddy boots. Hang it up on a pole in the trailer and transfer it to a row of nails in your headquarters as soon as possible. At the end of the shoot, choose a nice clean brace for each gun (guests first, of course) seeing that the birds are not tough, smashed by shot or crunched by hard-mouthed dogs. This is not so easy as it might appear, and I became aware of recriminations the following week when I discovered I had handed out less than satisfactory birds which, though they had looked alright at the time, turned out to have various defects. After that, I let everyone choose their own, so they had only themselves to blame if anything was wrong.

Whatever is left over must be sold to aid the financial situation. Keep a good brace in hand for the farmer – this is most

A good rushy corner; a mallard retrieved

important. Others who have done you favours, such as providing corn, saving nests or other such good turns should also have a brace, if not at the first shoot then as soon as you have any good ones to spare. The game dealer will take what is left over, but in practice you will find that the guns will buy most if not all of the surplus. You should charge the current wholesale price but you can apply discretion in the case of sub-standard specimens. A game dealer's licence is required if you sell game privately. If any gun should bag something unusual such as a woodcock, a teal or a mallard on a pheasant shoot, he should receive it as a tribute to his prowess and good fortune.

A pleasant little refinement is to produce a game card at the end of the shoot. A friendly printer will print a great pile of these cheaply enough, and someone must be deputed to write them out each time. One side will have a list of guns and the date and will be headed by the name of the shoot. On the reverse will be a list of the game shot and a total. This is a pleasant little token and a reminder of the occasion.

NOVEMBER

Another problem which might not be recognised as such will suddenly be thrown in your lap just when you least expect it. 'Alright if I bring a guest next time?' someone will ask just as you are going home. You will, if you are wise, have reached a commonly agreed policy on this matter some months before and you should each have a written set of rules so that all is clear. People can become touchy on the subject unless you are careful. I heard of a shoot in East Anglia which adopted a very liberal guest policy, if it could be called a policy. Quite simply, if you could not come or a better invitation turned up, you simply sent a substitute. This worked if one or two guns sent guests, but in time the guests came to outnumber the regulars. One day only one regular gun came – all the rest were guests. A series of near misses, a couple of pellets put into a beater and a dreadful day were the result. The shoot folded up, the keeper resigned on the spot and it was all rather sad.

It is equally easy to be Draconian on the subject and make it all but impossible for guests to be sent. Such was our over-cautious

A woodcock can make someone's day or even season!

Woodcock should be given to those who shoot them. A right and left such as this is a very rare and fortunate occurrence

policy at Duke's Ground in the first season. It was revised twice thereafter until the following set of rules was adopted. Everyone seems to think they are fair and they work. Those starting shoots might care to consider them:

1. No more than two guests per shoot.
2. First come, first served for guest bookings.
3. Each gun may have a second guest slot only when a guest vacancy occurs.
4. The host gun should try to accompany his guest, may not carry a gun and should act as an extra beater. If he cannot come, he must arrange with another gun to look after his guest. In this case, he should send a beater, as usual.
5. The onus is on the host to see that the guest is a safe and reliable shot and has been fully briefed as to the nature of the shoot, local customs and so on.

This seems to cover most situations and, with an element of give and take, everyone is happy. It is a mistake to become too bogged-down with rules and pettifogging regulations, but people like to know where they are, and a few rules are not only essential, they help things to run smoothly. To run a shoot, you need to be something of a politician and a public relations man combined.

One point about shooting days which is sufficiently important to merit a special mention is the matter of safety. Just like bad drivers, you will never meet anyone who admits to being an unsafe shot, although there are enough of them to be seen when you go out and about. Each season there is a catalogue of gun accidents varying from the odd pellet to a fatality. Your ambition is to avoid any such occurrences, but you must be realistic enough to know that accidents happen in the best company. They result from carelessness, from complacency, from bad habits, from mechanical failure, from being too keen (ie greedy) a shot or sometimes from 'Acts of God'. The shoot captain can eliminate most of these by choosing his guns carefully in the first place. No one is immune from the occasional slip and few shooters can claim never to have fired a dangerous shot; even

Try to produce high, fast birds

fewer can report never having witnessed a potentially lethal situation in the shooting field. Incidents which you see or which may be reported to you may be dealt with quietly at the time by having a gentle word with the guilty party. While that word might be gentle, it must also be firm. There is generally too much pussyfooting about this matter and people in authority shirk their duty of saying the 'hard word'. You owe it to everyone else in the field to do the right thing and the culprit will accept the criticism in the way it was offered, and if he does not you would probably rather not shoot with him anyway.

One rule which will help is to have a clear 'unload' whistle at the end of every drive and another, equally unmistakable, sign to show when the shooting may recommence. Other risky moments are shooting 'down the line', following through a neighbour, entering and disembarking from vehicles and all those times when attention wanders and an accident is the last thing in the mind. Safety is a vital facet of any shooting day and the captain for the occasion must acknowledge his responsibility to see that the rules are observed.

12
December

Stops – cocks only – poachers – alarm guns – straying – gratuities – Boxing Day shoot – wildfowl – various

This month ought to see your best shoot. By the second week the farm root crops, if any, will be all but gone and you are left with your little patches of game cover, ditches and hedge bottoms and any pieces of woodland you may be lucky enough to possess. The birds will have flown a few times, will have worked out some escape routes, will be faster on the wing, will be fewer, but will also be concentrated in the last remaining patches of cover. Natural food will still be available but will be sparser by the day and heavy feeding is vital at the hoppers and feed stacks. Change or freshen the straw as it becomes muddy and soggy. You may decide, after all, that you can begin to emulate grander shoots and place a few stops some time before you drive. A few small boys each armed with a stick, a warm coat and a packet of sweets can be placed at hedges and ditches which run towards your cover. Their job is merely to wait there, tapping occasionally, to prevent pheasants which have fed there in the mornings from wandering out into the fields and from departing even more hastily when the shooting party arrives. This is a boring job, as anyone who has done it will testify, so you will have to devise some suitable rewards for those who do it.

Your best shoot should be conducted according to the pattern which should, by now, have become familiar. Perhaps you will take special care with the cover that you have grown or the wood that you have so carefully preserved. All your planting, feeding and caring which has taken you so much time and so many resources, is now, we hope, to be justified. The effort you made

Sugar beet, even near houses, is a good game and holding crop

to plant your strips of kale and mustard way back in May will surely now be vindicated, for they represent the only patches of cover left in an otherwise bleak landscape.

If the season has been a success in breeding and releasing, it will not be until some time this month that you impose the 'cocks only' policy. If there is any doubt about stocks, impose it sooner rather than later. The latest theory that a good number of cocks in spring, each with its own territory, will call in your neighbour's hens is still not proved. Old-timers never shot a hen after Boxing Day, believing that the basis for any shoot was the number of breeding hens left at the end of the season. On a wild bird shoot I believe in the truth of this and a restriction placed at the proper time will be your insurance for the following year. Your policy, remember, is to build up the stock of game on your ground and not start virtually from scratch every February.

December is also a month in which shoots tend to be struck by poachers. The modern poacher is often an expert and is efficient and ruthless on big shoots, bagging hundreds of birds in a night rather than tens. The usual method is to shine a light at roosting birds in trees, and shoot them down with a powerful air rifle. The odds on the poachers escaping with a clean pair of heels are good, and if ever they are brought to court the sentences they tend to receive bear little relation to the value of their haul. Many police forces seem unwilling or unable to combat the problem, although there are some rural policemen who are expert and efficient in dealing with it.

The full-time keeper spends nights out watching his coverts and alerts the police or other watchers by means of two-way radio if there is any sign of trouble. The do-it-yourself shoot is unlikely to have any members, however keen on helping they may be, who have either the time or the inclination for all-night vigils in the depths of winter. In fact, these are largely unnecessary as your birds are likely to be more scattered and much thinner on the ground than on the larger shoots. You are more likely to be 'hit' by the less professional poacher or car-window shooter. The latter is an evil about which little can be done unless you can witness him in action and write down his car number. Even then, you need a witness to ensure a successful prosecution. The opportunist who walks the fields in your absence is more likely to be a local man, possibly one who may be known to you. You can only warn him off, catch him red-handed or be so vigilant that he considers it no longer worth his while to come.

More positive deterrents take the form of regular visits to the shoot, especially at weekends and in the evenings, where you can be seen cruising slowly around in your car. A pair of binoculars will be useful, but if the poacher knows that at any time one of the shoot members is likely to be prowling round, it will make him nervous and less inclined to risk a visit. Time spent on this sort of surveillance is never wasted and it gives a chance to top-up feed hoppers, watch the behaviour of the birds and maintain a familiarity with the ground. Another trick is to use an alarm gun of the type sold for many years by Gilbertson and Page. On touching the all-but-invisible trip wire, there is a deafening explosion a few feet from the intruder's ear. Set an alarm gun in your most vulnerable places near feed rides and in woods, but put the trip wire high enough to be avoided by rabbits and hares. If you have deer on the ground you can only use an alarm gun away from their haunts. It is a strong nerved poacher who can withstand the shock to the system which this device produces. For all he knows, authority will be rushing to the spot at the sound. If an alarm gun is set off more than twice, move it, otherwise the poacher will learn to avoid it.

The farmer and his workers will also be useful, especially if they live on the spot, and with a small amount of conditioning and training on your part they will come to react to the sound of shots and come to investigate. It may be that, before your time, the land was regularly visited by pot-hunters, and the farmer and locals had become used to casual poaching. As soon as the news spreads that the farm is now in the hands of an efficient and resolute body of shooters many of these problems will vanish.

Another good deterrent to poachers is to interest the local police in your enterprise. The nature of their duties means that quite often one or two local constables will be free on your shooting days and might be keen to come and beat for you. I know a number of shoots where this happens. Once they have become interested and involved, they come to regard the place with a proprietorial air and never fail to glance across it as they drive past in their Panda cars, and will even drive down the farm road at night. Local villains soon recognise the signs and all but the most stubborn will desist from their nefarious practices. Another possibility is to enlist the help of potential poachers and make them allies instead of enemies. This must be done discreetly, otherwise you might find yourself with a viper in your

A good shoot captain/amateur keeper does his best to show good birds

bosom. On Duke's Ground we secured the aid of a teenage lad who might have represented a risk and he grew zealous in the protection of 'his' birds and took a keen interest in helping us with all aspects of shoot management. Had we sent him off with a warning, he might have become a very real threat. It has been said that the best poachers make the best keepers, and there is an element of truth in the old saying. To lose birds to poachers with their non-selective methods is a thing that no shoot will tolerate. Vigilance is the only answer, and complacency in the absence of hard evidence that you are being 'done' is a recipe for disaster.

This is, like the acorn season, another time of year when pheasants tend to stray, either in search of better food or to warmer cover than you have provided. In the past, some keepers had secret substances which they mixed in with the birds' food to make them remain. The concoction was usually a blend of aniseed, hemp and various aromatic oils, but the actual recipe was a closely guarded secret passed on from father to son in the strictest confidence. Each keeper had his own magic formula. Today there is still belief that the attractiveness of pheasant food may be increased by certain additives and there are those who swear that this is the answer. For those not blessed with an inherited secret mixture, Sta-put by Gilbertson and Page might be the solution. This is a conglomeration of various substances which have long been believed to hold game birds and it is used by many keepers to, they claim, good effect. However, there are also those who believe the whole thing to be an old wives' tale. All I can say is that we have used Sta-put on Duke's Ground and we seem able to hold our birds as well as anyone, but whether it is for that or for other reasons is impossible to say.

As Christmas approaches, you must do the right thing and distribute a few 'Christmas boxes' amongst those who have helped you during the year and who are not members of the shoot. Special cases must be the farmer himself, the farm manager, any farm worker who has been especially helpful, neighbouring farmers who may have allowed you to include their fields in

Shooting ground game can be dangerous; warn guns in advance if hares or rabbits are likely to be seen

certain drives and other vital helpers such as the head beater. Some of these will have received birds from you during the season but a mark of special thanks at this time of year is appropriate and is only a small gesture on your part in return for favours done with no expectation of reward and which may have made all the difference to your season. Your funds for this purpose will be limited, but you ought to be able to afford a bottle of warming liquor in keeping with the Christmas spirit! This is an important thing to do, and it should not be forgotten.

On Boxing Day, it is traditional practice to take part in some form of country sport. Some members of your shoot will be engaged with family commitments on that day but a few will be keen to show the flag. A late start and a gentle stroll round the boundaries, followed by a leisurely lunch, should be the order of the day. Keep out of the cover and concentrate on any forgotten or rarely visited corners. More than any other shoot, the Boxing Day affair is a social occasion. If you kill enough for each gun to take home a brace of something or other, you will have done well enough.

If you have any ponds on your shoot or a river running through it you may count yourself very fortunate. Wild duck are comparatively easy to attract to a piece of water, even quite a tiny patch, provided there are duck in the area. They have an uncanny ability to find food, and regular feeding with barley will develop a lead-in of birds. The corn should be placed in shallow water to prevent rats, moorhens and sparrows from stealing it. Once a lead-in of duck has been established, the place must be kept quiet, regularly fed and shot very lightly. A flight pond is a delicate bloom, easy to destroy by too much handling. Two guns once a fortnight is the absolute maximum you can afford on a pond, whereas a stretch of river with a constantly changing population of wildfowl can take rather heavier shooting.

Duck ponds respond to feeding, and can quickly become a feature of the shoot; do not overshoot

Duke's Ground beaters – loyal and keen

    To be fair to all guns, the duck shooting might be run on a rota system with a number of prescribed shoots being arranged, and a series of teams of two or three friends having a clear field. Try not to disturb your duck on pheasant shooting days. All birds shot should be recorded, date, species and number, so that a complete picture can be made when the season ends. Sometimes duck will glean fresh stubbles or frosted potato fields, in which case you will need an ad hoc arrangement as such chancy fowl are likely to have departed while you are making complex and long-winded arrangements. A few quick phone calls on the day before should enable you to assemble a team, but here again justice must be seen to be done and all members of the syndicate must be given an equal chance.

    Duke's Ground has two rivers, one on each of two of the boundaries. One river has a narrow 'wash' which floods in wet winters and which can be attractive to duck. We tried the rota system but some guns, through lack of interest or for reasons of distance, did not take advantage of the facility. We then tried a 'go-as-you-like' arrangement which has worked well and there has been no overshooting. However, whatever system you

DECEMBER

employ might need to be reviewed at short notice as conditions and members of the shoot change. The Game Conservancy publishes a useful pamphlet on duck ponds and it might be, if you are especially lucky with your landowner and he has a boggy end to a field, that he might allow you to construct your own pond there. Water on farms is a valuable commodity, especially with the boom in trout rearing and fly fishing, and you might be able to sell him the idea. Once that has been done, you might even try some duck rearing, which is a good deal more easy than pheasant rearing, and thus add another dimension to your shoot.

While pheasants and partridges might be expected to form the basis of your quarry, the do-it-yourself man does not ignore rabbits, pigeons, crows, jays and even moorhens which might be despised on the more traditionally run estate. Sport with a shotgun may be had at more than just game birds and the 'various' ought not to be neglected.

Ducks are a bonus on any shoot and should not be neglected

13
January

Feeding – cock shooting – the shoot social – planning next season

By the start of the new year the keeper, be he professional or amateur, feels that his season is as good as over and he is already thinking of the year ahead. On the shoot his duties will consist mainly of what he did in the previous February, feeding his remaining birds hard, looking after the hens which are so important to the coming year and keeping an eye on the vermin. Shooting will consist of chasing the cock pheasants in the remote corners and previously un-driven dyke banks where they have found refuge. This pastime will not require many beaters but good dog-men will be at a premium as the really old cock birds you are after are adept at running and hiding at the right times. If you have any duck this will be a good month for wildfowl as the harder weather bites and fresh flocks arrive on migration.

At the end of the season it is pleasant to arrange a social or a party of some sort for guns, beaters, helpers and their wives. The pub which has served you well, we hope, during the season might prove as good a venue as any. This is a pleasant way to round off your season, to review it, to assess where things went wrong, to recollect with pleasure where they went well and recall with mixed feelings all the hard work that you have done. This is also a time for planning of a general nature and discussion of that vital factor, improving the cover. Will you be able to sow your strips next season? Now is the best time to transplant more shrubs and bushes and thicken the elder clumps while the sap is lying dormant. Running your own shoot will give you a clear idea of how a full-time keeper occupies himself and an apprecia-

Even the most modest shoot needs at least one picker-up

tion that the job may never be said to have been completed.

The end of the month will be the time for an important meeting with the farmer. You hope to be invited to continue to rent the shooting or whatever arrangement you negotiated twelve months before. The farmer will have his own ideas on how you have treated the land, whether you have left piles of empty cartridge cases, peppered his stock, damaged fences, forgotten him at Christmas, been discourteous to farm workers, shot his favourite cat or other heinous acts. If you have been guilty, do not be surprised if he wishes the experiment to cease. If, on the other hand, you have regarded yourselves as guests on his land and acted accordingly he will probably ask you to continue. This might be the occasion to suggest a five-year arrangement for the reasons of incentive and continuity which occurred to you when you embarked upon the venture. The guns will be more keen on tree planting and re-stocking if they know they are going to be around the following year to reap some of the benefits of their efforts.

If you have done all you can to be good tenants, the farmer

Dogs crowd into the guns' minibus; it is impossible to have too many dogs, providing they are well-behaved

might also feel able to make concessions so that the traffic is not all one way: a little more corn perhaps or some cover crops or maybe a tractor driver 'on the house' for shooting days. Something is sure to occur which will be mutually convenient. He may wish to increase the rent, and this is, of course, his prerogative. If you have killed few birds due to your policy of restraint and sparing hens, this might be unreasonable of him. Once your bags have begun to build up, a higher rent might become more appropriate. If a five-year agreement is reached, then the rents should be set now, so that you are able to make some costings and long-term estimates of financing, charges to guns and other matters. Details of the bags for the first four years on Duke's Ground Shoot and a typical balance sheet for the year are given in Appendices 5 and 6.

It may be that there will be some changes in your team of guns. Ideally you would prefer a consistent group so that the individuals become familiar with their responsibilities on the shoot and know each other well. This cannot always be so. Some guns may decide your shoot is not for them, may have better offers, come into the money to afford something more ambitious and less arduous or move away from the area. Remaining members are sure to be able to recommend suitable replacements. It may even be that a member has to be asked to leave the team for his persistently dangerous shooting, his failure to enter into the spirit of things or other pressing reason. This is a distasteful and delicate task and the do-it-yourself shoot captain's powers of diplomacy will be taxed by such a job. If that member leaves with no ill feelings and with the belief that he is acting in his own best interests, the shoot captain may feel entitled to give himself a large clap on the back. There is no point in hurting people's feelings unnecessarily. However, the sooner a firm team for the next season is established, the better.

If you have achieved your object, you will have enjoyed a season of sport on ground where there was little or none to be had before and now the place is much better endowed in terms of stock, cover, rearing and keepering equipment than it was when you took over. If you can say this at the end of every January for the first five years, you will know that you are on the right lines.

Now the scene is set for you to embark on a new season of motivating guns, organising days, killing vermin, feeding, making pens, collecting eggs, shooting pigeons, socialising, negotiating, book-keeping, planting maize and the countless other little jobs which are the lot of the do-it-yourself game shooter. Nearly all of it is fun, otherwise no one would do it.

Appendix 1

Gilbertson and Page Limited

This firm is probably the chief supplier of aids to the keeper and they offer a wide range of useful equipment and materials at competitive rates, promptly delivered.

We used, with success, the following items from their catalogue, available from them at Corrys, Roestock Lane, Bowman's Green, St Albans, Herts:

Fenn vermin trap
Mink trap (gated)
Fox snares
Upright alarm gun
Renardine vermin repellent
Poult pellets
Maintenance pellets
4-gallon drinking fount
Feed hoppers
Marking rings
1in netting for pens
Sta-put non-stray mixture
Canary grass seed
Maize
Oyster shell grit
Gapex
Resitex

Appendix 2

The Game Conservancy

This is the main organisation in the country devoted to the furtherance of shooting, conservation and farming jointly, and the development by research of the most effective ways of rearing, holding and feeding gamebirds and creating habitats suitable for their needs.

APPENDICES

Game Conservancy Advisory Booklets

Game and Shooting Crops
Wildfowl Management on Inland Waters
Partridge Rearing and Releasing
Pheasant and Partridge Eggs – Production and Incubation
Diseases of Gamebirds and Wildfowl
Farm Hazards to Game and Wildlife
Pheasant Rearing and Releasing
Game Records
Grouse Management
Feeding and Management of Game in Winter
Woodlands for Pheasants
Predator and Squirrel Control
Roe Deer
Red-legged Partridge
Grey Squirrels
The European Woodcock
Rabbit Control
Game Conservancy Annual Reviews

This body also markets various keepering aids and shooting equipment which the do-it-yourself man may find useful. All information and prices can be obtained from the Game Conservancy, Fordingbridge, Hampshire.

Appendix 3

Monthly Newsletter

An example of a monthly newsletter, which is useful for keeping members thinking as a team and a good way of passing on information:

October

Dear Fellow Shooter,

Good to see everyone at the working party last week. It is nice to think that our pen sections are safely stored away until next year. The rearing season was generally successful and we lost only fourteen poults which were 'bad do-ers' to start with. The birds are staying well in covert and the four white ones we put down are showing up proudly, suggesting that there has been little straying. Please keep the feeding rota going; although there are plenty of stubbles, the birds must learn where there is a regular supply. Don't forget to top up the drinkers.

One fox was snared on the path to the big pen. That makes four this year. Vermin tally is now at forty-two head which has been a real contribution by our three vermin trappers to the welfare of the wild birds which are also showing well, now that the corn is cut.

Preparations are now in hand for the first shoot, partridge and cock pheasants on 15 October. Meet at the usual time with your one or two beaters, preferably one with a dog. Lunch will be at HQ and the pub has been arranged as usual for after the shoot.

Shoot bar: John has this in hand and has bought stocks. There will be a levy of £2 per gun per shooting day to defray his costs. Liquid contributions are, of course, welcome at any time. He will also be running a sweepstake of the possible bag on the day.

Guests: There are still a few vacancies for the December shoots. Please let me know if you wish to avail yourself of the facility. As usual, first come, first served.

There will be a clay shoot on the morning of Sunday 28 October. Meet at HQ and the shoot will take place on the stubble next door where it will cause least disturbance.

Transport: We are grateful to have once again the use of Dick's trailer which is so useful to us on shoot days.

Please continue to collect all the corn you can. We are well down on last year's tally. All offerings should be left in the 40-gallon drums at HQ to prevent the rats spoiling it.

See you on the 15th: hoping for a good day.

Yours sincerely,
J.

Appendix 4

Automatic Feeders

The part-time keeper is hampered both by his amateur status and the lack of time. He may be an accountant or a builder whose professional affairs very properly fill the large part of his working hours. In winter and early spring he leaves his house before dawn and returns after dark; his keepering duties are therefore limited to weekends, night patrols or some lamping for vermin. If we accept that a vital part of building up any shoot depends on winter feeding, then there is an obvious problem. Self-feed hoppers have their advantages as does the feed stack – a pile of gleanings thatched with pieces of straw bale is useful, but sparrows and rats will quickly discover such places and turn them into slums, and much of your corn will be wasted.

The Parsons Mark III Automatic Game Feeder

One answer is the automatic feeder. These are most useful when feeding game poults in summer when, by simple Pavlovian training, they learn to respond to the call at an early stage. However in January, when natural food is at its shortest, such a gadget can help a full-time keeper with a distant wood, while to the absentee amateur keeper it can be a godsend.

Of the growing number available I will highlight three which incorporate most of the important points. The principle is simple enough, involving a vermin-proof hopper which, at pre-arranged times, will scatter regulated amounts of corn or pellets for game birds. It will be standing out for most of the year, and must be utterly reliable, as two or three missed feeds will have some of your birds foraging elsewhere. It should require a minimum of servicing, for regular keeper visits will defeat the object of the exercise. It should not cost so much as to break the budget of a modest do-it-yourself set-up. It should be easy to operate, and have the capacity to vary the times, amounts and numbers of feeds in a twenty-four-hour cycle. In an ideal world, it would not jam with fragments of straw or small clods in your feed, but it should be able to distribute corn or pellets with equal ease.

Three feeders now on the market incorporate many of these features. Probably the best known is the Parsons Mark III Automatic Feeder. It has a voluminous, 2cwt hopper – less topping-up is required, but it is quite tall, so that it can be a struggle for a shortie to lift a sack of corn to head height to tip it in. It is made from galvanised steel, and designed with drip rings to prevent rain-water gathering in vulnerable spots.

There is a tightly fitting lid, stout, splayed legs for stability and feet to prevent it sinking into soft ground. A simple clockwork timer, specially modified, allows any number of feeds per day so that poults which require food little and often and mature birds eating corn in winter may be equally well served. The amount of food released per feed is varied by a simple dial which has the effect of shortening or lengthening the spinning time.

Pellets or grain are scattered over a 6yd radius, preferably onto straw, and no vermin can steal food from the hopper. Power is provided by a 12v car battery connected by two leads with crocodile clips. It is wise not to leave trailing wires as pheasants try to perch on them and pull them out. A spare battery is also useful so that one may be on charge while the other is in situ, thus preventing breaks in feeding. One fully-charged battery will last for about six weeks, but clearly this will vary depending on length and frequency of feeds. The Parsons feeder has been giving service for over twelve years and has proved its worth. When the specially pitched horn sounds, pheasants weaned on it come running and flying from two or three fields away. On a short feed, the horn continues to sound after the spinner has stopped, allowing late comers to home-in on the spot. The Parsons has also been used effectively to feed trout and deer. When used on a flight pond, one side of the spinner may be masked so that the grain is scattered in the shallows and not on dry land for the rats and moorhens.

Operating on a similar principle is the East Anglian Shooting Products Automatic Feeder, designed by John Storry of that firm. More portable but smaller (48in high and weighing 56lb when empty) than some other makes and made of glass-fibre, the keeper does have the option of bolting an extension onto the 4cu ft (200lb) hopper. The spinner is of novel design and operates more on the principle of the fertiliser spreader, flicking the food from 706sq ft to 1,590sq ft with considerable lever power. The working parts seem to be rather exposed to the weather: ice in the spindle of any feeder will damage it and wet pellets can set to the consistency of cement. If the keeper is concerned about this, he can easily make a rain guard from a dustbin lid with a 6in hole cut in the middle and inserted the right way up into the bottom of the frame. Unlike the Parsons, this feeder has a light sensitive eye so that whatever settings you have made, it reacts to the first glow of dawn and feeds 30 minutes later. This is useful as dawn breaks at different times according to the weather and the season, and an automatic feed at that time will arrive before the pheasants have strayed out for breakfast. The daylight cycle can be set for amount (18–90 seconds) and regularity on a simple, two control console on one leg of the feeder. The cycle ends when darkness falls and all is ready to start again next morning. Power is the usual 12v battery and corn or pellets may be fed; straw and

The East Anglian Shooting Products Automatic Feeder

small twigs not proving a problem. For heavy feeds, the spinner may be lowered by means of a wing nut. The simplicity of construction is an attractive feature but, like the Parsons, the colour is rather conspicuous – pure white. In my view, the fewer people who see your feeder standing out boldly in a cover strip, the less likely they will be to fiddle with or vandalise it. The EASP bleeper or constant pitch call is a thin but penetrating shriek and, like that on the Parsons, it can be heard by pheasants a surprising distance away.

The third feeder which is creating interest is one produced on a cottage industry basis (only to order) by Richards Staines of Newark. The object of this model was to cut costs and still give a reliable service without necessarily producing a feeder of the aesthetic and graceful lines of the other two. Based on the excellent rubberised plastic 40-gallon rain or chemical barrel, this feeder is the least attractive of the three. However, its homely exterior hides sound electronics and rugged workmanship and, like the EASP feeder, it starts its daily cycle at dawn when the photo-electric cell, coupled to printed circuits and microchips, sets off the first feed after which manual programming is possible.

The RGS Mark II Automatic Game Feeder has three splayed legs made of 1in box section steel and a lockable lid to the hopper. Feeding time is variable from 5–90 seconds on a graduated scale. To counteract the criticism that such sophisticated hardware is beyond the capabilities of many amateur keepers, the timer has its own power source (two long-life dry batteries), which removes the possibility of coupling the battery terminals back to front. The high-pitched bleeper has a volume control on a manual slide type of baffle, which avoids placing an extra drain on the battery.

The RSG Mark II is made to order, and you must allow about a month for delivery. A more costly glass-fibre version is still in the planning stage.

The Parsons Automatic Feeder, Mark III: available from Parsons, Blackfriars Road, Nailsea, Bristol, BS19 2BU, Avon, for about £280 plus VAT.

The East Anglian Shooting Products Automatic Feeder (without hopper extension): available from EASP, London Road, Attleborough, Norfolk, for £200 inc VAT.

The RGS Mark II Automatic Game Feeder: available from Richard Staines, 102, Hollies Avenue, Newark, Notts, for about £175.

Appendix 5

Bags on Duke's Ground Shoot

Bags for the first four years:

	Year 1	Year 2	Year 3	Year 4
Pheasant	73	198	267	506
Partridge	2	15	37	42
Wildfowl	11	32	3	61
Woodcock	2	3	2	1
Pigeon	12	17	20	11
Hare	3	5	9	9
Moorhen	15	19	14	6
Various	7	7	11	14
Total	125	296	363	650

All game shot on formal shooting days only.

Year 1 pheasants, cocks only.

Wildfowl numbers depend on wetness of the season and consequently flooding of river 'washes'.

There is still room for improvement and the shoot has not realised anything like its full potential. Year 4 also happened to be a very good wild bird year.

Appendix 6

Balance Sheet

Income	£	Expenses	£
10 guns at £200	2,000	Loss on last season	32.00
10 guns at £10 supplement	100	Rent	1,795.72
3 guns (non-working) at £70 supplement	210	Kale seed	16.00
		Poults at £1	300.00
Sale of game	92	Ex-laying pen birds at £1	100.00
	2,402	Roll of wire	39.55
		Pellets	25.79
		Diesel	5.00
		Gratuities	22.80
		Postage	11.00
		4 beaters at £3	12.00
		Various	10.20
			2,370.06
		Cash in hand	31.94
			2,402.00

This assumes donations of corn, wood for making pens, some cover crop seeds, shrubs and bushes, Fenn traps, other materials and all labour and travelling expenses.

Appendix 7

The Shoot Secretary

It is best if, as team leader, you handle the roles of treasurer and shoot secretary yourself, and deal with all the paper work. Bearing in mind the principles of good management, there might be a case for employing a member of your team who possesses administrative skills but, on balance, the extra time required to communicate decisions and pass and receive funds means that these tasks can be done more efficiently by one person, preferably the shoot captain, in whose name the lease will be.

The shoot secretary must be a good organiser, used to basic office management systems. He must be confident in handling other people's money and must maintain a meticulous system of accounting. Various people are regularly pushing small sums of money into his hand, usually at inconvenient times, and they also expect re-imbursement for expenses which he may or may not have authorised.

He must be sure that all matters of insurance are properly handled, for claims may be made against him in the event of an accident where someone is shot, injured by a shoot vehicle or suffers a similar mishap. If negligence is proved the organiser is liable, so your tight organisation on the shooting day must be backed up by all the proper insurances. The BASC membership, which includes third party insurance, should be a condition of carrying a gun, but the secretary should also check the farm policies regarding accidents to authorised persons, and be sure of his responsibilities under the Health and Safety at Work Act for, on a shoot day, he is employing beaters whether or not they are paid in cash.

If game is to be sold, he must possess not only a game licence, available from the Post Office (as must the other guns), but also a licence to deal in game which is available from the local Council. The guns will hold shotgun certificates, but he must be sure that they are up to date. He should be aware of the Law relating to guns on the highway and consequently be quite clear which farm roads, if any, are classified as public rights of way.

He will order poults and cover crop seeds and negotiate with the farmer when and where they are to be drilled. Everything involving cost must be carefully considered with the help of trusted and experienced advisors in order to keep expenditure, and hence the subscriptions paid by the guns to a minimum.

He will also write, duplicate and post the newsletter, keep the game book up to date, see to the printing of game cards, the distribution of Christmas gratuities, sale of game and negotiations with neighbouring landowners. His public relations work is important and he must be on good terms with his neighbours, their keepers and shooting tenants as well as with farm workers. He may have to contact the local police in the case of poaching and must keep a list of the registration numbers of suspicious cars.

It is essential for the shoot secretary to possess a telephone and be able to do some basic typing. He will need to think of everything the others may well forget. Although this list may seem formidable, the task need not be a burden if the jobs are carried out promptly and efficiently. Allow things to slide and the job will become a misery and the shoot will suffer. The shoot secretary, whether or not he doubles as field captain, has a key role without which the enterprise cannot succeed.

Further Reading

The British Association for Shooting & Conservation. *Handbook of Shooting: The Sporting Shotgun* (Pelham, 1983)

Coats, Archie. *The Amateur Keeper* (Andre Deutsch, 1978)

Douglas, James. *Gundog Training* (David & Charles, 1983)

– *The Sporting Gun* (David & Charles, 1983)

The Game Conservancy. *The Complete Book of Game Conservation* (Barrie & Jenkins, 1975)

Hastings, Macdonald. *The Shotgun: A Social History* (David & Charles, 1981)

Humphreys, John. *Modern Pigeon Shooting* (Tideline Books, 1980)

Humphreys, J. (ed). *The Shooting Handbook* (Beacon Publishing, 1983)

Irving, Joe. *Training Spaniels* (David & Charles, 1980)

Jackson, Tony. *Shotguns and Shooting* (Ward Lock, 1981)

Luxmoore, Edmund. *Deer Stalking: The Whys and Wherefores* (David & Charles, 1980)

Marchington, John. *Shooting: A Complete Guide for Beginners* (Faber & Faber, 1972)

Moxon, P. R. A. *Gundogs: Training and Field Trials* (Popular Dogs, 1981)

Thomas, Gough. *Shotguns and Cartridges for Games and Clays* (A. & C. Black, 1975)

Index

Numbers in *italic* refer to photographs

accidents, 113
acorns, 100–101
advertising, 22
alarm gun, 119, 130
artichokes, Jerusalem, 46
automatic feeders *see* feeders, automatic

bags, typical, 8, 137
BASC, 85, 139
beaters, *3*, 83–5, *84*, 88–9, 90, 94, *95*, *124*
BFSS, 63, 85
Boxing Day shoot, 122–3
brails, 75–6
brooder, paraffin, 61
butts, portable, 94–6, 99

cats, 37–8
'Christmas boxes', 121–2
clay shoots, 63
coots, *34*
corn
  feeding, 25–6; *see also* feeders, automatic; feed hoppers; feeding;
  obtaining, 27, 83, 104;
  storing, 27–8, 83
costs, 8, 9, 18, 29, 31, 84, 98, 138
cover
  improving, 15, 126;
  planting, 15–16
crops, cover, 17, 44, 46, 48, 56, 65, 87, 93, 106;
  cutting, 72–3;
  drilling, 44–6, 48;
  spraying, 48, 101
crows, 17, *33*, 34, *35*, 36, 125

deer, 119
dogs, 59, *62*, 63, *64*, 72, 84, 94, *128*
drilling *see* crops, cover
drinkers, 52, 54, 77, 130

drives, planning, 17, 88–91, 94, 96
ducks, 83, 123–5, *123*, *125*, 126

eggs
  collecting, 49–50, 59–60;
  rearing from, 29
exchange services, 12, 20–1

farmer, relationship with, 11, 12, 16, 17, 32, 42–3, 45, 56–7, 109, 119, 127
feather-pecking, 78, 80
feeders, automatic, 27, 81–2, 132–4, *133*, *135*, 136
feed hoppers, 25–7, *26*, 32, 54, 130
feeding, 7, 52, 71, 77, 77–8, 80–2, 91, 103–4, 116;
  in pens, 52;
  sites, 23–4, 91;
  systems, 24–5
feed stack, 24–5
feed storage, 27–8, 71, 83
Fenn trap, 21, 38–40, *39*, 41, 54, 69, *70*, 130; *see also* traps
ferrets, *56*
first shooting day, 94, 99–100
flags, 94, 99, 106
flight pond, 123
flushing bar, 59
footpath, 71–2
foxes, 17, 36–7, *37*, 40, 67, 69, 71

game
  card, 110;
  count, 16;
  dealer, 110;
  diary, 102;
  handling and distribution, 109–10;
  licence, 139
Game Conservancy, 25, 48, 60, 76, 130;
  publications, 35, 41–2, 61, 82, 125, 131

INDEX

gapes, 82
Gapex, 82, 130
gas, Cymag, 38, 71
gibbet, 55
grit, 54, 68, 71, 130
guests, 97, 111, 113
guns
  choosing the, 17-19, 21-2;
  number of, 18, 19;
  placing of, 88, 96, 97, *105*

hare shooting, 9, 90, *122*
harvest, 72-3, 74
hawks, 35
hay-cutting, 49, 57, 59
headquarters, shoot, 28-9
hedgehogs, 37
hen birds *see* pheasants
hens, broody, as rearers, 60
hides *see* butts, portable
home rearing, 29, *51*, *53*, 59-61
hoppers *see* feed hoppers

incubators, 60-1
insurance, 85, 139

kale, 46, 48, 65, 106, 117
keepers, 7, 15, 18, 19, 20-1, 30, 55, 61, 74, 82, 90, 118, 121, 126, 132
kestrel, *41*

land, finding suitable, 9-11
landowner, approaching the, 11, 12
lease, terms of, 12, 85
leg rings, 76, 130
lunch, shoot, 97-8

maize, 46, 65, 130
mallard, *42*, *47*, 83, 110, *110*
mink, 38
modern game shooting, 7-9
moorhens, *34*, 35, 125
mustard, 46, 48, 117

nest box, 60
nests, 49, *49*, 50, *50*, 59, 79
newsletter, 42-3, 131-2

owls, 35

partridges, 16-17, 55-6, 83, 86-7, 88, 94-5
pegs, 96-7, *97*
pellets, feeding
  breeder, 77;
  maintenance, 77, 130;
  pheasant, 71;
  poult, 54, 80, 130;
  turkey, 71
pen birds, ex-laying, 75-9, *81*
pens, release, 50-4, 65-9;
  equipment for, 50-1, 52-4, 68-9;
  siting, 65-6
pheasants
  cocks, 16, *30*, 106, 117, 126;
  hen birds, buying, 30-1;
  hen shooting, 104-5;
  rearing systems, 29-30, *51*, *53*;
  shooting days, 104-6
  straying, 121
pickers-up, 85, *87*, *101*, *127*
pigeons, 56-7, 125
poachers, 118-19, 121
poison, 36, 38
potatoes, 48, 101
poults
  buying, 30, 50, 79-80;
  feeding, 71, 80-2;
  releasing, 82;
  rearing, 29-30, 61
predators, 33-42, 55

rabbits, *38*, 57, *57*, *58*, *122*, 125
rats, 27, 38, 69, 71, 75
rearing policy, 29-31, 50; *see also* home rearing
releasing
  points, 65-6;
  programme, 50, 75-9
releasing runs *see* pens, release
Renardine repellent, 71, 130
rent, 12, 18, 127, 128
ringing *see* leg rings
rooks, 34

safety, 113, 115

142

INDEX

shoot
  captain, *91*, 100, *120*, 129;
  first day, 94, 99–100;
  mapping the, 15;
  potential of, 15;
  secretary, 138–9;
  size of, 11
shooting dates, establishing, 85–8
sick and injured birds, 80, 82
silage-cutting, 49, 57
snares, 40, 54, 69, 71, 130
sparrow guards, 25, 26, *28*, 54, 69, 93
Sta-put non-stray mixture, 121, 130
stoats, 17, 37, 38, *38*, 39, 67, 83
stops, 116
storing equipment, 28–9, 93
straw, 27, 68, 74–5, 83, 104;
  for feed stack, 24–5
stubble-burning, 17, 74
sugar beet, 48, 66, 87, *117*
supper, shoot, 107, 109
syndicate, forming a, 17–18, 21–2

tagging *see* wing tags
team
  changes in, 128–9;
  operating as a, 62, 63

tenancy, renewing, 127–8
theft, 66
transport, 96
traps
  cage, 34–5;
  Fenn, 21, 38–40, 41, 54, 69, 130;
  inspection of, 40–1, 55;
  lines of, 40;
  setting, 38–40;
  see also snares
trespassers, 72

'unload' whistle, 115

vermin, control of, 15, 17, 32–3, 38–42, 44, 55, 69
vermin book, 102

Warfarin, 71, 75
weasels, 17, 37
wheat, 104
white game birds, 103
wild broods, 71, 73
wing-clipping, 75
wing tags, 76
woodcock, 110, *111*, *112*
wormer, gamebird, 82